THEORY
OF
CONSTRAINTS

What is this thing called

THEORY
OF
CONSTRAINTS

and how should it be implemented?

Eliyahu M. Goldratt

North River Press
Great Barrington
Massachusetts

Additional copies can be obtained from your local bookstore or the publisher:

The North River Press
Publishing Corporation
P.O. Box 567
Great Barrington, MA 01230
(800) 486-2665 or (413) 528-0034

www.northriverpress.com

Manufactured in the United States of America

Library of Congress Cataloging-in-Publication Data

ISBN: 0-88427-166-8

To Dale Houle who, during a long week in Israel, forced me to dictate to him this entire book. He has carefully and thoroughly managed the difficult task of editing the text and correcting my English without distorting the message.

Only such a capable, bright person and such a very good and warm friend could have done all that while continuing his fully booked teaching schedule. If there ever was an author who could say "without this person this work would have never seen light," I certainly can say it about Dale.

Table of Contents

Introduction

In 1985, *The Goal* was introduced into the market. Initially, it encountered a lot of skepticism—a management textbook written in the format of a love story? It will never be accepted.

That was the opinion of most "experts," but as usual, they were wrong. *The Goal* was not just a book about a success story, it became a success story itself! Read and cherished by CEOs and floor workers, by hard-nosed professionals and housewives, its impact was beyond my wildest expectations. Not only that, this "love story" became mandatory reading in numerous universities. It is probably one of the very few fiction books that turned into an accurate documentary.

Hundreds of plant managers all over the globe have identified so strongly with the hero—Alex Rogo—that they have replicated his actions and thus his astonishing results. Testimonials of those occurrences have streamed in from all over in the form of letters, telephone calls and numerous enthusiastic personal stories. And, they still come in—more than ever.

But these implementation efforts, along with their tangible results, have exposed two major obstacles. Obstacles that in almost all cases, have caused the companies' results to plateau and some times even decay. It turned out that any improvement, no matter how big, is not sufficient. Only a process of ongoing improvement can sustain a company's excellent performance in the long run. Sounds quite trivial, but its ramifications are far from being trivial.

Very quickly it became evident that *The Goal* is not providing what is actually needed. *The Goal* provides brilliant simple solutions when what is really needed is the process that will enable management to generate such solutions on their own. Moreover, *The Goal* may have highlighted, but certainly did not address, the major problem of changing the nature of a company. Changing it to the extent that change itself will become the norm, not the exception.

This is certainly a psychological problem that requires not just the know-how of dealing with the psychology of individuals, but more important and more difficult, the know-how of dealing with the psychology of the organization.

This book is written in the attempt to deal with these two major questions: what are the thinking processes that enable people to invent simple solutions to seemingly complicated situations? How can we use the psychological aspects to assist, rather than impair, the implementation of those solutions in a mode of an ongoing process?

Realizing full well that this book, if it is to be effective, must be studied and not just read, I hope that *The Goal* will be of help as a vivid illustration of the generic methods described here.

E. M. Goldratt

PART ONE

What is this thing called

THEORY OF CONSTRAINTS?

1. *The Five Steps of Focusing*

The message of this book is not bottlenecks or cutting batches. It's not even how to arrange the activities of the factory floor. As a matter of fact, the message is the same for any aspect of any company from product design and marketing to manufacturing and distribution. Everyone knows that the actions of marketing are guided by the concept of cost and margins, even more than the actions of production. And everyone knows that the best salesman in his/her company is the one who violates all the rules—which immediately implies that the rules in marketing are as wrong as those in manufacturing.

If we don't bother to verbalize our intuition, we ourselves will do the opposite of what we believe in.

We grossly underestimate our intuition. Intuitively we do know the real problems, we even know the solutions. What is unfortunately not emphasized enough, is the vast importance of verbalizing our own intuition. As long as we will not verbalize our intuition, as long as we do not learn to cast it clearly into words, not only will we be unable to convince others, we will not even be able to convince ourselves of what we already know to be right. If we don't bother to verbalize our intuition, we ourselves will do the opposite of what we believe in. We will "just play a lot of games with numbers and words."

How do we listen to what we intuitively know to be right?
How do we go about verbalizing it?

The first step is to recognize that every system was built for a
purpose. We didn't create our organizations just for the sake of
their existence. Thus, every action taken by any organ—any part
of the organization—should be judged by its impact on the overall purpose. This immediately implies that, before we can deal
with the improvement of any section of a system, we must first
define the system's global goal; and the measurements that will
enable us to judge the impact of any subsystem and any local
decision, on this global goal.

Once these are defined, we can describe the next steps in two
different ways. One, in which we are using the terminology of
the system that we are trying to improve. The other, using the
terminology of the improvement process itself. We find that
both descriptions are very helpful and only when both are considered together, does a non-distorted picture emerge.

*In our reality any
system has very few
constraints.*

How to sort out the important few from the trivial many?
The key lies in the recognition
of the important role of the
system's constraints. A system's constraint is nothing
more than what we all feel to be expressed by these words:
anything that limits a system from achieving higher performance
versus its goal. To turn this into a workable procedure, we just
have to come to terms with the way in which our reality is constructed. In our reality any system has very few constraints (this
is what is proven in *The Goal,* by the Boy-Scout analogy)* and at
the same time any system in reality must have at least one constraint. Now the first step is intuitively obvious:

* See Appendix 1.

1. Identify the System's Constraints.

Once this is accomplished—remember that to identify the constraints also means to prioritize them according to their impact on the goal, otherwise many trivialities will sneak in—the next step becomes self-evident. We have just put our fingers on the few things which are in short supply, short to the extent that they limit the entire system. So let's make sure that we don't waste the little that we have. In other words, step number two is:

2. Decide How to Exploit the System's Constraints.

Now that we decided how we are going to manage the constraints, how should we manage the vast majority of the system's resources, which are not constraints? Intuitively it's obvious. We should manage them so that everything that the constraints are going to consume will be supplied by the non-constraints. Is there any point in managing the non-constraints to supply more than that? This of course will not help, since the overall system's performance is sealed—dictated by the constraints. Thus the third step is:

3. Subordinate Everything Else to the Above Decision.

But let's not stop here. It's obvious we still have room for much more improvement. Constraints are not acts of God; there is much that we can do about them. Whatever the constraints are, there must be a way to reduce their limiting impact and thus the next step to concentrate on is quite evident.

4.　Elevate the System's Constraints.

Can we stop here? Yes, your intuition is right. There will be another constraint, but let's verbalize it a little bit better. If we elevate and continue to elevate a constraint, then there must come a time when we break it. This thing that we have elevated will no longer be limiting the system. Will the system's performance now go to infinity? Certainly not. Another constraint will limit its performance and thus the fifth step must be:

5.　If in the Previous Steps a Constraint Has Been Broken, Go Back to Step 1.

Unfortunately, we cannot state these five steps without adding a warning to the last one: "But Do Not Allow Inertia to Cause a System Constraint."

We cannot overemphasize this warning. What usually happens is that within our organization, we derive from the existence of the current constraints, many rules. Sometimes formally, many times just intuitively. When a constraint is broken, it appears that we don't bother to go back and review those rules. As a result, our systems today are limited mainly by policy constraints.

Their original reasons have since long gone, but the policies still remain with us.

We very rarely find a company with a real market constraint, but rather, with devastating marketing policy constraints. We very rarely find a true bottleneck on the shop floor, we usually find production policy constraints.* We almost never find a vendor con-

---

* This by the way is the case described in *The Goal.* The oven and the NCX-10 didn't really lack the capacity required to supply the demands. Alex didn't have to buy a new oven or a new NCX machine. He just had to change some of the production policies that were employed in his plant.

straint, but we do find purchasing policy constraints. And in all cases the policies were very logical at the time they were instituted. Their original reasons have since long gone, but the old policies still remain with us.

The general process thus can be summarized (using the terminology of the system we seek to improve) as:

1. Identify the system's constraints.
2. Decide how to exploit the system's constraints.
3. Subordinate everything else to the above decision.
4. Elevate the system's constraints.
5. If in the previous steps a constraint has been broken, go back to step one, but do not allow inertia to cause a system constraint.

As we said before, the only way not to cause severe distortions, is to describe the same process, but this time using the terminology of the improvement process itself. Every manager is overwhelmed with problems, or as some would call it opportunities. We all tend to concentrate on taking corrective actions that we know how to take, not necessarily concentrating on the problems we should correct and the actions needed to correct those problems. Thus, if a process of ongoing improvement is to be effective, we must first of all find—WHAT TO CHANGE.

In other words, the first ability that we must require from a manager is the ability to pinpoint the *core* problems, those problems that, once corrected, will have a major impact, rather than drifting from one small problem to another, fooling ourselves into thinking that we are doing our job. But once a core problem has been identified, we should be careful not to fall into the trap of immediately struggling with the question of How To Cause The Change. We must first clarify to ourselves—TO WHAT TO CHANGE TO—otherwise the identification of core problems will only lead to panic and chaos.

Thus, we should also require that a manager acquire the ability to construct simple, practical solutions. In today's world, where almost everybody is fascinated by the notion of sophisti-

cation, this ability to generate simple solutions is relatively rare.
Nevertheless, we must insist on it. It's enough to remind ourselves of what we have so harshly learned from reality, over and
over again. Complicated solutions don't work, simple one's
might. Once the solution is known, and only then, are we facing
the most difficult question of—HOW TO CAUSE THE
CHANGE.

2. The Process of Change

Struggling and surviving these politics gives us a deep intuitive understanding of the psychological processes involved.

If the first two questions of WHAT TO CHANGE? and TO WHAT TO CHANGE TO? are considered to be technical questions, then the last one, HOW TO CAUSE THE CHANGE? is definitely a psychological one. However, we are very well prepared for such questions. In our organizations there is generally more than just a little bit of politics. Struggling and surviving these politics gives us a deep intuitive understanding of the psychological processes involved. What we have to do is to *verbalize* these processes.

We all know, especially in the light of the last few hectic years, that a process of change—the way we've tried to induce it—cannot be expected to be a short one. To change an organization takes, unfortunately, years. It is a frustrating process for everyone involved and many times demands severe "casualties." It's enough just to review the process of the five steps described earlier to realize the magnitude of this problem. Identify the constraints, exploit, subordinate, elevate, go back . . . and then go back again . . . and again.

What we want to implement is a Process of Ongoing Improvement, where change is not an exception but rather the norm. Where change is ongoing, we must be much more methodological in our approach to the improvement process itself, otherwise it is just a matter of time until we give up and the organization will once again stagnate. So let's start to verbalize what we already know:

> Any improvement is a change.

Not every change is an improvement but certainly every improvement is a change.

We cannot improve something unless we change it. Anyone who has worked in an organization for even a few months knows that we cannot escape the validity of the following step:

> Any change is a perceived threat to security.

There will always be someone who will look at the suggested change as a threat to their own security.

Now the door is wide open for the unpleasant conclusion. What is the unavoidable result when you threaten somebody's security?

> Emotional resistance!

Anybody who thinks we can overcome an emotional resistance with logic was probably never married. We can only overcome emotion with a stronger emotion.

Let's summarize once again this devastating process that connects improvements to emotional resistance.

> Any improvement is a change.

Leading to:

> Any change is a perceived threat to security.

Leading to:

> Any threat to security gives rise to emotional resistance.

Leading to:

> Emotional resistance can only be overcome by a stronger emotion.

What emotion are we trying to trigger in order to induce change in an organization? Maybe the best way to clarify it to ourselves, is to describe here, one of the most popular and well founded approaches (even though far from being effective).

Imagine yourself standing before the management of your company. You are trying your best to highlight to them that we are living in an unprecedented era in Industrial History. The demands, placed by the market on our capabilities, are increasing at an almost exponential rate.

You bring, for example, the quality issue and you demonstrate how your clients are continuing to tighten their minimum requirements every year. Today, the minimum quality requirements are such, that just five years ago they were thought to be an impossibility.

Then you bring up the increased demands being placed on the company's product capabilities. Demands that cause a severe and accelerating shrinkage in your company's product life cycle. If this is not enough, then you will probably want to elaborate even more on the exponential increase in the pressure. This time you will dwell on something like the need for better due date performance—the percentage of times in which you fulfilled the orders on time. You are probably going to point out that 10 years ago a due date performance of 70% was acceptable. Today, scoring 90% is far from being satisfactory.

This same phenomena exists in quoted lead times. In spite of the fact that during the last years your company has been quoting shorter and shorter lead times, the pressure from the market to quote even shorter ones seems to increase rather than decrease.

Then you will probably want to summarize, graphically, how

Eliyahu M. Goldratt

all the demands placed on your company have increased in the last 20 years. Asking for forgiveness, from your audience, for not putting numbers on the vertical scale, you will draw a graph that looks something like the one in Figure 1.

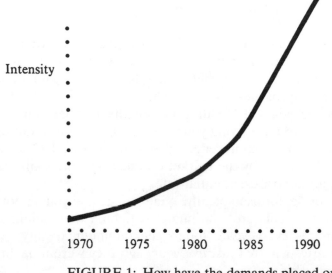

FIGURE 1: How have the demands placed on your company increased over the last twenty years?

After that, you will take another fresh transparency to overlay on the graph you just drew. Then, you say to your audience: "suppose we copy from our best competitor" (remarking that it's not so easy to keep pace) and choosing another color you will copy the same graph on the fresh transparency. Then you'll remind your audience that you are starting behind the competition with a gap of about two years. Saying that you will shift the new transparency to the right the appropriate number of years, creating on the screen a picture similar to the one shown in Figure 2.

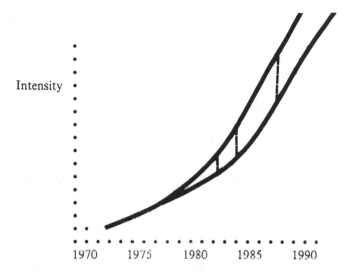

FIGURE 2: Suppose we do copy from our best competitors, how big will the gap be?

And then taking a large red marker you will highlight the gaps between the two lines, as they were six years ago, three years ago and now (coloring in the dotted bars in Figure 2). Turning to your audience you will probably say in a dramatic tone: "do we all understand the meaning of the increased gap?" Since the only response will be a murmur, you will try to use a joke to both ease the tension and strengthen the message.

Bob and Harry are going to Africa to hunt lions on a safari. They leave their Land Rover to track the lions by foot and three miles away from it, they find out that they ran out of bullets. Bob immediately sits down to take his boots off and put his sneakers on. Harry in an astonished tone asks him, "what the hell are you doing?" And Bob, in a very calm voice answers, "if a lion comes, I want to be able to run fast." Bursting into nervous laughter, Harry replies: "do you really think you can run faster than a lion?" just to turn pale when Bob's calm response is, "of course not, but I don't have to run faster than a lion, I just have to run faster than you."

Putting jokes aside, ask yourself: what is the emotion that we are trying to trigger by such a presentation? If it wasn't clear before, now it is certainly obvious. We are using fear and insecurity. We are trying to overcome the immediate insecurity resulting from change, by provoking the long term insecurity of what will happen if we don't change. We are fighting fire with fire. But let's not forget, whenever we use fire to fight fire somebody gets burnt. To use such an emotion in order to constantly sustain a process of ongoing improvement, a process where change is the norm, means that we have to constantly create an environment of insecurity in our organizations. Do we really want it? Is that the environment we want to work in?

Besides, is this approach effective at all? It might be effective for the top guys for whom the future is a reality. But as we move down into the organization it is clear that the effectiveness of the long-term threat diminishes rapidly. As a result, we have to revert to more tangible threats, like "do it or else."

we will rapidly find ourselves in the position of the kid who shouted "Wolf" too many times.

Even if this method of forcing insecurity—in the name of "we must improve or else"—works initially, we must also understand that its effectiveness will diminish as time goes by. Simply because, if it is initially effective and we do improve, then the bad ramifications that we predicted will not materialize and we will rapidly find ourselves in the position of the kid who shouted "Wolf" too many times. To sustain a process of ongoing improvement we must find another way to constantly induce change. So we better go back and re-examine the logic that connects improvement to emotional resistance, in order to find a flaw in it. Some way to break the grip of this seemingly untouchable logic.

"Any improvement is a change," granted. But what about the second link, "any change is a perceived threat on security," for everybody? Our experience immediately supplies the answer. No, the suggested improvement is not a threat to everyone. It is certainly not a threat to the one who suggested the improvement. He/she doesn't see any threat in the change, they just see the good ramifications that will stem from the improvement.

Maybe the best way to understand this phenomena is to relate it to our own personal experience. Almost all of us have come, at one time or another, with an idea of how to improve something. I'm not talking about trivialities, I'm talking about those cases where we were troubled by a problem for many, many weeks or maybe even months. And then one morning the light bulb went on. The solution was so obvious that we couldn't understand how we hadn't figured it out long ago. Then we came to work all charged up. We gathered our peers, our people (as a matter of fact, anybody that we could put our hands on) and controlling our enthusiasm as much as we could, tried to explain logically what now seemed to us to be just a common sense, obvious solution.

Do you recall what was the immediate reaction? Before you even finished explaining, the response was probably something along the lines of: "we're different, it won't work here." This is just the emotional resistance to change that was explained earlier.

Let's concentrate on our own behavior, the behavior of the one who suggested the change. Usually, when placed in such situations, we don't give up so easily. We fight for our ideas. What is the emotion that we are radiating? Are we totally logical? Think how everybody, our peers and our subordinates, must have related to our idea as they talked amongst themselves. They probably used phrases like, "be careful, this is Johnny's baby." We were radiating emotion to the extent, that they probably referred to our idea as *OUR BABY*.

Where improvement is concerned, more than one emotion is present. Not just the emotion of resisting change, but the very powerful emotion of the inventor. This last emotion is so powerful that sometimes one inspired person will overcome the resistance of many. Can we utilize the emotion of the inventor—the emotion which is based on the meaning in life, rather than on seeking security? The emotion of let's do what makes sense.

Can we utilize it to induce a change, an ongoing change, in an organization?

Where improvement is concerned, more than one emotion is present. Not just the emotion of resisting change, but the very powerful emotion of the inventor.

At first sight it looks quite hopeless. Where are we going to find those individuals? Moreover, how can we prevent the erosion that will undoubtedly occur from the constant struggle with the mammoth waves of regenerated resistance. Using this emotion on a grand scale will just mean that we have to induce everyone in our organization to invent the same thing at approximately the same time. That looks even more ridiculous. Still the emotion of the inventor is so positive and so powerful that maybe we should give it more thought, before we decide to give up and revert back to our usual way of using the carrot and stick method.

What is the minimum that is required for a person to gain the emotion of the inventor, the ownership of an idea? Is it necessary for the person who invents the idea to be the first one to do it in the world? Or is it enough for this person to just invent it for themselves? Nobody told them, they figured it out all by themselves. Maybe in such a case, it is also okay if this person is very well aware of the fact that others have invented it before? The mere fact that they figured it out for themselves may be sufficient to take ownership, to be the inventor. Your experience probably indicates that this might actually be the case.

But, even if it is, another problem will immediately surface. How can we induce someone to invent a solution to a specific predetermined problem? There once was such a method, which we still refer to as the Socratic method. But is this 2,500-year-old method still applicable in our modern times? Thus the two main questions are now:

1. Does the emotion of the inventor arise whenever a person is figuring out an idea for themselves, even though they know that others have already figured it out?
2. Is the Socratic method still applicable in our modern times?

In order to answer these last two questions, we have conducted a grand scale analysis. To make sure that the results would be decisive, the analysis is such that if the positive emotion of the inventor is not triggered, then by default, the opposite emotion—that of hate, will be.

But there is one thing that we simply cannot tolerate—constructive criticism.

What causes us to hate someone? If that person does something to us that we don't particularly like. Most of us don't like to be criticized. Vicious criticism, we like even less. But there is one thing that we simply cannot tolerate—constructive criticism. Constructive criticism means that there is something correct in the criticism. It's under the belt. It's unfair. We are certainly going to hold it against the one who criticized us for a long time.

The analysis that we have conducted probably included you as well, so you will be able to testify, first hand, to the validity of its results. The analysis is of reaction to the book *The Goal.* "*The Goal* is nothing new. It is just verbalizing clearly what we already knew, just common sense."

At the same time *The Goal* is a criticism, almost a condemnation of the way we ran our plants in the past. And it is constructive criticism, since it is outlining a practical way out—simple, practical solutions. Judging by the response of most of its readers—by its surprising popularity—it is quite evident that *The Goal* didn't raise the emotions of hate but rather much more positive ones. Did we succeed to use the Socratic method to trigger the emotion of the inventor?

The Goal was written using the Socratic approach and that's the reason why it's a novel. The novel format was not used as a sales gimmick, it is simply essential when using the Socratic approach. To induce someone to invent, you must bring him/her—at least mentally—into a realistic environment. That is why all the books that were written in the Socratic way, including the original dialogues of Plato, were written as novels.

In *The Goal* there is a character called Jonah. Jonah seems to be really nasty, especially when Alex Rogo comes to him practically begging and pleading for the answers. The reader knows very well that Jonah has the answers. But he doesn't give them to Alex. Instead he gives Alex the questions. And when Alex eventually figures out the answers, then Jonah gives him . . . even more questions. Almost all the readers were somewhat irritated by this approach, "what are all these games?, give the answers!"

If what you want is action to be taken, then you must refrain from giving the answers.

Just ask yourself, about the outcome, had Jonah given Alex all the answers at the outset? Intuitively we know that Alex would never have gone and implemented them. So, at least, we have learned one thing, don't give the answers.

The minute you supply a person with the answers, by that very action you block them, once and for all, from the opportunity of inventing those same answers for themselves. If you want to go on an ego trip, to show how smart you are, give the answers. But if what you want is action to be taken, then you must refrain from giving the answers. *The Goal* deliberately elaborates on Alex's struggle to find the answers, so that the intuition of the reader will have sufficient time to crystalize. This is so the reader will figure out the answers before he reads them. Readers have usually been, at least, one page ahead of Alex Rogo throughout the book. Is *The Goal* successful in doing this?

We certainly didn't ask all the readers if this is actually what happened to them, but we do have good reason to believe that this is what was accomplished. *The Goal* is also a textbook used formally in hundreds of universities all over the world. You don't expect that people will voluntarily read a textbook from cover to cover in less than a week. Nevertheless, the common reactions of the readers are, "I finished it in two or three sittings"; "I couldn't put it down." Why does this happen? *The Goal* is certainly not an exceptionally good piece of literature. Most probably it happens because the readers are inventing the answers before they read them and that's why they couldn't put it down. The urge to verify, to yourself that you are right, is an almost uncontrollable urge.

Now to the crucial question. Did the reader, by inventing the ideas in *The Goal* (before reading them), take ownership? Let's remind ourselves that this is exactly what we wanted to check. Is the emotion of the inventor triggered, even in cases where the person knows that somebody else has already invented the same thing before—which is certainly the case with the readers of *The Goal?*

To answer this question, just ask yourself the following. Did I, after finishing reading *The Goal,* feel almost compelled to give it to someone else?

We know for a fact that this is very often the case. You see, *The Goal* was not originally made available through bookstores (even today it is quite rare to find it in a bookstore). Nevertheless the mechanism of people passing it, actually forcing it on each other, is so strong that many hundreds of thousands of copies of *The Goal* have been sold.

The results are very decisive. People are much more open than we tend to think and their intuition is extremely powerful. Everybody has the ability to invent, if skillfully induced. And once people invent something for themselves, they actually take ownership. Another result, of this same analysis, is that the Socratic method is extremely powerful, even in our modern times.

The immediate question is: how to formally use the Socratic method? Let's remember that when *The Goal* was written, it was guided by intuition and not by formalized rules. Any research in literature reveals that an ocean of words have been written about the Socratic method. But we—in spite of all our extensive efforts—could not find, in this vast amount of material, even a clue of how to actually use it. But before we dive into the enormous subject of using the Socratic method, it might be worthwhile to summarize the three steps of the Theory of Constraints. The steps which are equivalent to the above five steps, but are expressed in the terminology of the improvement process itself:

1. What to change?
   Pinpoint the core problems!
2. To what to change to?
   Construct simple, practical solutions!
3. How to cause the change?
   Induce the appropriate people to invent such solutions!

We even know the method that will enable us to accomplish the third step—the Socratic method. Let's try to verbalize the rules that comprise the Socratic method. When we are trying to induce someone to invent a solution, for a problem which is under their control, the first step that must be accomplished is quite obvious. We must make sure that the problem we present to our audience will be regarded by them as their problem—a major problem of theirs. Otherwise how can we even hope that they will commit their brains to attempting to solve it? This all sounds quite convincing and it's probably even right, but how are we going to convince someone that a particular problem is theirs—how can we prove it to them?

Remember there are two things which are working against us when we try such a thing. The first is the natural tendency of any person to react to such a situation by claiming, it's not their problem or at least he/she is not the one who caused it and thus cannot do anything to about it. The second is the fact that the usual way to prove something is simply not effective in this case. We are used to proving things by "the proof is in the pudding" method. But when you try to bring people to realize their own problem, you certainly cannot use their pudding. Using their pudding means to solve and implement for them. So, in using this method we will have to bring examples of other people's "puddings." The pilot method. Look here, they had the same problem and see how they have solved it. We all know what the common response is to such presentations: "we are different, it won't work here," the puddings are not always the same.

3. *How to Prove Effect-Cause-Effect*

A way which does not rely on examples or references but on the intrinsic logic of the situation itself.

The first stumbling block that we face in using the Socratic method is thus, the need to formulate another way to prove things. A way which does not rely on examples or references but on the intrinsic logic of the situation itself, which is by far more convincing than the usual methods. This method of proof is called Effect-Cause-Effect and it is used extensively in all of the hard sciences. The following is an extract from the *Theory of Constraints Journal* that describes this generic method in detail.*

Everyone who has spent some time in an organization has probably asked himself whether managing an organization is a science or does it border more on the side of an art? The more time one spends in an organization and the more a person climbs toward the top of the pyramid, the more he seems inclined to believe that managing an organization is more of an art than an accurate science. The art of managing people. The art of reaching intuitive decisions when hard facts are not available. The art of

* Volume 1, Number 2, Article 2.

often managing in spite of the existence of numbers that others, less experienced, think are hard facts.

It is almost a consensus today that since we are dealing with so many unknowns in an organization that this field will never be a science. The unpredictable reaction of the market, the unknown actions of our direct and indirect competitors, the changing reliability of our vendors—not to mention the constant stream of internal "surprises"—all combine to defeat any attempt to approach the subject in a "scientific" way. Some—and they certainly are not a small group—even claim that since organizations comprise human beings whose reactions cannot be scientifically predicted, it is an absurdity to hope that the subject of managing an organization can be turned into a science.

Is this really so? I believe that any attempt to answer this question must first establish what is meant by "science." Does the word science carry with it the premise of having a precise answer for every situation? Is it a collection of well established procedures? Or is it the glorified and somewhat mysterious notion of "finding the secrets of nature?" Not surprisingly, science—for most people—is a blend of all of the above. This muddled view stems from the fact that the various sciences did not spring up as fully developed subjects. Rather each science has gone through three quite distinct and radically different stages of development. In each stage every science completely changes its perspective, nomenclature and even its intrinsic premise, much like a caterpillar turning into a worm in its evolution to becoming a butterfly.

The three distinct stages that every science has gone through are: classification, correlation and Effect-Cause-Effect.

The three distinct stages that every science has gone through are: classification, correlation and Effect-Cause-Effect. Let's clarify these stages through some examples. Probably one of the most ancient sciences known to man is astronomy. The first stage—classification— begins in prehistory. Several classifications of the stars were developed according to their location in the heavens. The most popular one was invented by the ancient Greeks. They segmented the sky to twelve sectors called the signs of the zodiac and classi-

fied the stars according to these sectors. Within this broad classification they invented an elaborate subclassification, coloring the
night sky with their vivid imaginations and succeeding to etch
above us most of their stormy mythology. Some stars they ob-
served "refused" to stay in one sector, so they classified these
wandering stars in a class of their own—the planets. This mammoth effort had its own practical use. It created a common terminology and today it still has some use in navigation, even though
we must admit that its principal use is in horoscopes.

The second stage started with Ptolemy in Alexandria about two
thousand years ago. This wise man postulated the first known
correlation on this subject. The planets move along a circle, whose
center moves along another circle, whose center is the earth. This
correlation has been improved upon by others, who have more
precisely pinpointed the radii of the circles and even added more
circles to an already quite complicated model. These efforts certainly bore fruits. They enabled us to predict eclipses and to forecast the position of the planets in tomorrow's skies.

The correlation stage is not a stand-still stage. It has its turbu-
lences and fierce debates. Copernicus aroused a somewhat sleepy
community by his daring suggestion that a much more powerful
correlation would be achieved and if we put the sun as the center
of the planet's orbits. Kepler created another turbulence by sug-
gesting a correlation based on elliptical orbits rather than the
almost holy circular ones. It should be noted that in the correlation stage, even though it is based on careful observations and
often involves substantial mathematical computations, the question WHY is not asked at all. Rather the question HOW is the
center of interest.

The man who moved this subject into the effect-cause-effect
stage is known to everybody—Sir Isaac Newton. This man was the
first to insist on asking the question: WHY? He had the courage
to ask it not only about remote planets but about seemingly mun-
dane day-to-day events. Why do apples fall down rather than flying in all directions? How easy it is to shrug off such a trivial
question by the impertinent answer—"that is the way it is." Newton didn't; instead he assumed a cause for this phenomenon. He
assumed the gravitational law. He suggested that if we assume
that any two bodies attract each other in proportion to their
masses and in reciprocal proportion to the distance between them

squared, then we can logically explain many effects in nature. Because of his assumption (the gravitational law), three of Kepler's correlations were explained for the first time and eight more were exposed as just coincidences that had not been thoroughly checked. With Newton's assumption of a cause the word *explain* appears on stage. It is a foreign word to the classification and correlation worlds where the only "proof" is in the pudding. Try it, it works.

Not surprisingly, the effect-cause-effect stage opened a whole new dimension. We are no longer just observers tracking what already exists in nature. We can now predict the orbit of satellites that we ourselves add to space. Past experience is no longer the only tool. Logical derivations based on existing assumed causes can predict the outcome of entirely new situations.

It's worthwhile to note that, before Newton, astronomy was not considered a science. As a matter of fact the name used at that time is the best indication—astrology. Even Kepler was an astrologer (and mathematician) and had to supply his king with weekly horoscopes. Only when the third stage is reached, only when cause-and-effect is established and logical deductions/explanations are suddenly mandatory, do we fully recognize that a subject matter is a science.

Let's examine another subject—diseases. The first stage—classification—is mentioned as far back as the Old Testament. When certain symptoms are present—put a quarantine on the house, when other symptoms exist—isolate the person, and with yet other symptoms—don't worry about them, they won't spread because of contact with the person. Diseases were classified not only by their symptoms but also by their ability to infect others. This stage was certainly very helpful. It served to localize diseases and prevent them from spreading. The second stage—correlation—was achieved only in the modern world. Edward Jenner found that if serum is transferred from an infected cow to a human being, this human being would not be infected by smallpox.

Immunization had been found. We were no longer limited to just preventing the spread of the disease. In one specific case we even prevented and eventually eliminated it. But once again the question WHY was not asked. The only proof was "try and see." No wonder that it took over seventy years before Jenner's methods were generally accepted.

The man who moved us into the Effect-Cause-Effect stage was Louis Pasteur. He said: Let's assume that those tiny things that Leeuwenhoek found under his microscope more than a hundred years before, those things we call germs, are the cause of diseases—and bingo microbiology sprang to life. Bingo, of course, means many years of hard work for each disease. By having a cause-and-effect we could now create immunizations for a very broad spectrum of diseases. Yes, not just find immunizations, but actually create immunizations, even for those diseases where such immunization is not created spontaneously in nature.

But the most important stage—the one that is by far more powerful because it enables us to create things in nature—is the stage of effect-cause-effect.

We can go over each subject that is regarded as a science, whether it is chemistry, genetics or spectroscopy, and the pattern is the same. The first step was always classification. There are often some practical applications from this stage but the major contribution is usually to create the basic terminology of the subject. The second step—correlation—is usually much more rewarding. It supplies us with procedures that are powerful enough to make some practical predictions about the future. Mendeleev's table and Mendel's genetic rules are examples of this important stage. But the most important stage—the one that is by far more powerful because it enables us to create things in nature—is the stage of effect-cause-effect. Only at this stage is there a widely accepted recognition that the subject is actually a science. Only then does the question WHY bring into the picture the demand for a logical explanation.

Today there are quite a few mature sciences that have been in the third stage of effect-cause-effect for many years. The debate of what is a science is basically behind us. There is a consensus among scientists that science is not the search for truths or the search for the secrets of nature. We are much more pragmatic than that. The widely accepted approach is to define science as the search for a minimum number of assumptions that will enable us to explain, by direct logical deduction, the maximum number of natural phenomena. These assumptions—like the gravitational law—can never be proven. Even when they can explain an infinite number of phenomena this does not make them true. It simply makes them valid. They can still be disproved. One phenomena that cannot be explained makes the assumption false, but in doing so it does not detract from its validity. It simply puts the boundaries on the circumstances where the assumption is valid and exposes the opportunity to find another assumption that is even more valid. Science does not concern itself with truths but with validity. That's the reason why everything in science is open for constant checks and challenges.

Accepting this general view of science, let's turn our attention to the field of organizations. Certainly we see many phenomena in organizations. It would be quite ridiculous to consider these phenomena, that we witness every day in any organization, as fiction. They are no doubt a part of nature. But if all these organizational phenomena are phenomena of nature, which of the existing sciences deals with them? Certainly not physics, chemistry or biology. It looks as if this is an area waiting for a science to be developed.

If we narrow our focus to a subset of the subject of managing organizations, the logistical arena, we can easily trace the three stages. The first one crystalized in the last thirty years. We refer to it under the generic name of MRP (Manufacturing Resource Planning). It is now evident that the real power of MRP is in its contribution to our data bases and terminology and much less to its original intent—shop floor scheduling. Bills of material, routings, inventory files, work-in-process files, order files—all are nomenclatures brought by MRP. Viewed from this perspective it's quite clear that MRP is actually the first stage—classification. We have classified our data, putting it into clearly defined categories. We have created the basic language of the subject and tremendously improved communications.

The West invested considerable money, time and resources in the classification stage. On the other side of the globe, the Japanese moved almost directly into the second stage—correlation. One man was the major force behind it—Dr. Taichi Ohno. He started his career as a foreman and recently retired as the Executive Vice President of Production for all of Toyota. He is the inventor of the Toyota Production System and the Kanban approach. He is the inventor of the powerful correlations that we call Just-In-Time. Correlations like: if products are not needed downstream—as indicated by the lack of Kanban cards—it is better for the company that the workers stay idle or, cut the batch sizes of parts even if the cost of setup skyrockets. I received the best proof that the question WHY was not asked at all from Dr. Ohno himself. He told me in our meeting several years ago in Chicago, "My system does not make sense at all, but by God it's working." The best sign of the correlation stage—the only proof is in the pudding.

> *Common sense is the highest praise for a logical derivation, for a very clear explanation.*

Have we evolved already into the third stage, the effect-cause-effect stage? My answer is, definitely yes. Most of *The Goal* readers claim that this book contains just common sense. Common sense is the highest praise for a logical derivation, for a very clear explanation. But explanations and logical derivations are the terminology of the effect-cause-and-effect stage. In *The Goal* only one assumption is postulated—the assumption that we can measure the goal of an organization by Throughput, Inventory and Operating Expenses. Everything else is derived logically from that assumption.

The *Theory of Constraints Journal* is intended to expand this cause-and-effect logic to cover other aspects of an organization—from marketing, to design, to investment, to distribution, and so on. This is the main task of the first article in every issue. The task of the second article in each issue is quite different. The purpose of this article is certainly not to give real life testimonials that the Theory works. Who would be helped by such testimonials? The people that have already been persuaded by *The Goal* do not need them, they have their own real-life proof. Those who were not moved by the common sense logic in *The Goal* will certainly find it easy to demonstrate that their situations are different and that these ideas will not work in their environment. No, the purpose of the "Visit" articles is quite different. What is not well appreciated is that the effect-cause-and-effect stage brings with it some significant ramifications that we have to adjust to. It involves a different approach to untieing a subject. It also gives us the ability to change the system in which we operate, but in doing so it obsoletes for a while our intuition on how to operate in this new environment. In addition, and not less important, it demands a much more pragmatic approach to newly created "sacred cows." The second article's task is to deal with all these subjects. Let's elaborate on these points.

First, how do we usually approach a subject today? The first step is typically—let's get familiarized with the subject. We are thrown into the mammoth task of assembling information. We try to collect as much relevant data as possible. Sometimes it takes a while to identify what is actually relevant. Often times it's quite frustrating to discover how difficult it is to get reliable data. But usually, determination, effort and time enable us to put our arms around an impressive collection of relevant pieces of information. Now what?

Our usual tendency is to start arranging things. To put some order into the pile of information that we worked so hard to assemble. This is not a trivial task and certainly it takes time and effort. In most cases there is more than one alternative way to systematically arrange the data. It's not at all easy to choose between the various possibilities and too frequently we decide to switch in mid-stream between one systematic approach and another, throwing the entire effort into one big mess. The most frustrating part occurs toward the end when we are always stuck with some pieces of information that do not fit neatly into our system. We twist and bend, invent some exception rules and in the end it is all organized. What have we actually achieved? Classification!

Many times we call the above task a "survey." But it is customary to finish surveys with findings. Many of these "findings" turn out to be just statistics that we verbalize or present in a graphic form. This statistic, that "finding," is a direct result of our classification and sub-classification efforts. But let's not treat these statistics lightly. In many cases they are quite an eye opener. Nevertheless, most of us will feel uneasy in finishing such a mammoth job with just statistics. We are eager to get more concrete things out of our work. To accomplish this we usually screen the statistics looking for patterns and common trends between the various graphs and tables. We are looking for correlations. Usually we find some, but everyone who has been involved in such an effort knows that there are two problems with these correlations.

The first is that even when we find quite a clear-cut correlation we are still haunted by the suspicion that it might be a coincidence. The only way to get some verification is to perform an experiment. To deliberately change one variable and to closely monitor another to find out whether or not it changes according to the prediction indicated by the correlation.

The second and more serious problem is that we don't understand why the correlation exists and are always haunted by the possibility that the correlation involves more variables than what we have identified or that we haven't identified the known variables narrowly enough. Numerous examples of the first case are well known. Unfortunately the second case is more common and carries with it a larger problem. If a variable was neglected in a correlation, it will not take long until it emerges or we decide to declare the correlation invalid. Unfortunately, this is not the case if the variables were not defined narrowly enough. Most experiments will prove the validity of the correlation, but its implementation will involve a lot of wasted effort.

This correlation was broadcast as "Inventory is a liability."

A classic example of this problem is the correlation between a company's level of inventory and its performance. The surveys taken in the late seventies and early eighties indicated that the Japanese carried substantially less inventories than their Western counterparts. It also was very clear that the overall performance of these Japanese companies was superior to ours. This correlation was broadcast as "Inventory is a liability."

It is hard to overestimate the impact that this correlation had on Western industry. A frantic race to reduce inventories started. We are now in the midst of this race even though our financial statements have not yet caught up. They still penalize—in the short run—every company that manages to substantially reduce its inventory. The amazing thing is that this widespread effort has occurred without most participants having a clear picture of why it is important to reduce inventory. We still hear the usual explanation of investments tied up in inventories, carrying costs and interest cost. These cannot be valid explanations since the level of these factors has not changed significantly from ten years ago when inventory was still considered an asset.

The disturbing thing about this movement is that we have not distinguished which portions of inventory are really responsible for the improved performance. A very close scrutiny, as can be found in *The Race,* reveals that the reduction in the work-in-process and finished goods portions of the inventory is the prime reason for improvement in a company's performance. Raw material inventory reductions are shown to have a relatively small impact. Nevertheless, due to lack of this understanding many companies are paying their dues to the current crusade by leaning on their vendors, in order to reduce their raw materials inventories. In general most correlations are extremely helpful. The inherent limitation of any correlation is due to the lack of understanding of the cause-and-effect relationships between the variables connected by the correlation.

As we can see, the current approach of assembling information as the first step in approaching a subject leads us down the classification path, which may eventually evolve into fruitful correlations. Unfortunately this path fails to trigger the effect-cause-effect stage. In order to appreciate this, let's examine how a researcher in one of the established sciences operates. When such a person becomes aware of a new effect, the last thing that he desires at this stage is more information. One effect is enough. The burden now is on the scientist's shoulders. Now he needs to think, not to look for more data. To think, to speculate, even if in thin air. To hypothesize a plausible cause for this effect. What might be causing the existence of this effect? When such a cause is finally speculated the real task begins. The scientist must now struggle with a much more challenging question. Suppose that the speculated cause is valid, what is another effect in reality that this cause must explain? The other predicted effect must be different in nature from the original, otherwise the speculated cause is regarded as just an empty phrase. The researcher must search then to see if this effect actually exists. Once a predicted effect is actually found (and in the established sciences it might involve years of experimentation) only then does the speculated cause gain the name of theory. If the predicted effect is not found, it is an indication that the speculated cause is wrong and the scientist must now search for another plausible cause.

Kepler had in his possession all the voluminous and surprisingly precise measurements that Tycho Brahe and his group gathered over several decades. By analyzing this data Kepler succeeded, after a mammoth mathematical effort of more than thirty years, to produce some correct correlations and some more mistaken correlations. Newton, on the other hand, started by examining one effect—why an apple falls down. He speculated the gravitational law as a plausible cause and derived from its existence a totally different effect—the orbits of the planets around the moon. Correlations do not trigger the effect-cause-effect stage. At most they shorten the time required to check the existence of some predicted effects.

This process of speculating a cause for a given effect and then predicting another effect stemming from the same cause is usually referred to as Effect-Cause-Effect. Many times the process does not end there. An effort is often made to try and predict more types of effects from the same assumed cause. The more types of effect predicted—and of course verified—the more "powerful" is the theory. Theory in science—unlike in the common language—must be practical, otherwise it is not a theory but just an empty scholastic speculation.

> *We should strive to reveal the fundamental causes, so that a root treatment can be applied, rather than just treating the leaves—the symptoms.*

Every verified, predicted effect throws additional light on the cause. Oftentimes this process results in the cause itself being regarded as an effect thus triggering the question of what is its cause. In such a way, a logical tree that explains many vastly different effects can grow from a single (or very few) basic assumptions. This technique is extremely helpful in trying to find the root cause of a problematic situation. We should strive to reveal the fundamental causes, so that a root treatment can be applied, rather than just treating the leaves—the symptoms. I myself usually elect to stop the process of finding a cause for a cause, when I reach a cause which is psychological and not physical in nature.

We believe that real life examples of applying this way of thinking to analyze a company—the "Visit" articles—will be very helpful in moving from the classification–correlation approach to the effect-cause-effect stage.

In using the Effect-Cause-Effect method we strive to explain the existence of many natural effects by postulating a minimum number of assumptions. If all the effects just mentioned are considered to be undesirable ones, then the proper name for these underlying assumptions is Core Problems. Thus one of the most powerful ways of pinpointing the core problems is to start with an undesirable effect, then to speculate a plausible cause, which is then either verified or disproved by checking for the existence of another type of effect, which must also stem from the same speculated cause.

Using this method also means that after having identified one undesirable effect the search for more information should be put on hold. Rather, we should now immerse ourselves in the speculation of a plausible reason, which can explain the existence of this effect. Then we should try to logically deduce what other totally different effect *must* exist in reality if the speculated reason is valid.

It's no wonder that when using this method in a dialogue, we will initially give the impression that we are jumping from one subject to another.

Only then, should we seek verification, not of the original effect but of the speculated one. It's no wonder that when using this method in a dialogue, we will initially give the impression that we are jumping from one subject to another. Remember, the only connection that exists between the subjects being discussed is the hypothesis which resides only in our mind.

The Effect-Cause-Effect method is not just a very powerful technique to be used only in finding the core problems, or to just convince the one that did the analysis, that he/she actually did pinpoint the core problem. By explaining the entire process of constructing the Effect-Cause-Effect logical "tree" we have a very powerful way to persuade others.

Let's examine an example which uses this technique of thinking—in Chapter 4 of *The Goal*. Alex has just told Jonah that the robots which were installed in two departments of the plant have increased productivity by 36%. The assumption that Jonah makes is that Alex, being the plant manager, is not doing something which is an artificial, local optimum. Thus the hypothesis is, that when Alex uses the word *productivity,* he knows what he is talking about. Therefore Jonah's next question is not directed to the specific tasks of the robots, their manufacturer or even their purchase price, but rather towards the verification of what should be a straightforward resulting effect. "So your company is making 36% more money from your plant, just from installing some robots?"

Not surprisingly, the answer is no. Alex, captured in his world of local optimums, thinks that Jonah is the one who is remote from reality. Jonah now has to develop and present an Effect-Cause-Effect tree using Alex's terminology, in order to show Alex why the hypothesis ("Alex knows what he is talking about") must be wrong.

If the plant had actually increased productivity this would mean that either the plant increased Throughput or reduced Inventory or reduced Operating Expense. There aren't any other possibilities. Thus Jonah's next question is, "was your plant able to ship even one more product a day as a result of what happened in the department where you installed the robots?" Notice that Jonah is very careful to make sure he uses Alex's—a plant manager's—terminology. Basically Jonah was asking whether or not Throughput was increased. The next question was "did you fire anybody?" In other words, was Operating Expense reduced. And the third question was "did your inventories go down?"

As expected, Alex, at this stage is under the impression that Jonah is jumping from one subject to another. But when Jonah ties it all together, Alex cannot escape the validity of the conclusion. It is quite easy now for Jonah to hypothesis a much better reason, "Alex is playing a numbers game," and productivity for him is just a local measure like efficiencies and cost. The unavoidable effects that will stem from managing a plant in this way is what Jonah tries to highlight by his next question, "With such high efficiencies you must be running your robots constantly?" When this is verified, Jonah now has a very high degree of assurance that all the other effects must also be in Alex's plant. So without further hesitation he firmly states "Come on, be honest, your inventories are going through the roof, are they not?" And then "and everything is always late, you can't ship anything on time." Logical, firm conclusions except for someone who does not use the Effect-Cause-Effect method, like Alex. Then the reaction is "wait a minute here, how come you know about these things?"

The Effect-Cause-Effect method is a very powerful technique when used to determine core problems. As a matter of fact, it is the only feasible technique that we know of to identify constraints, especially if it's a policy constraint that doesn't give rise to permanent physical constraints, but only to temporary or wandering ones. This same method also solves the problem of providing solid proof. Read *The Goal* once again; it portrays a constant unfolding of Effect-Cause-Effect analysis.

It turns out that people are very convinced by this type of analysis when they are introduced, not just to the end result, but to the entire logical flow: hypothesizing reasons, deriving the resulting different effects, checking for their existence and, when not finding them, changing the hypothesis and so on. If you called *The Goal* common sense then you have already testified to the extent to which this method is accepted as proof.

4. *How to Invent Simple Solutions: Evaporating Clouds*

as long as we think that we already know, we don't bother to re-think the situation.

Once the core problem is pinpointed then the challenge of using the Socratic approach is even bigger. Now the audience has to be induced to derive simple, practical solutions. The major obstacle to accomplishing such a task is the fact that people usually already have in their minds, the "accepted" solutions. Remember, we are dealing with core problems and typically core problems. They have usually been in existence within our environment for many months or even years—they do not just pop up. This provides us with the best indication that the perceived solutions are insufficient, otherwise the core problem would have already been solved. It is clear that the nature of human beings is such, that as long as we think that we already know, we don't bother to re-think the situation. Thus whenever we want to induce people to invent, we must first convince them that the "accepted" solutions are false, otherwise they will not think, they will just quote.

It's not unusual to find that the accepted solutions, which do not work, are solutions of compromise. Our observation is that whenever a core problem is confronted, it turns out that the core problem was already intuitively very well known (even

36

though not necessarily well verbalized) and already compromising solutions were implemented in an futile attempt to solve the problem. Inducing people to invent simple solutions, requires that we steer them away from the avenues of compromise and towards the avenue of re-examining the foundations of the system, in order to find the minimum number of changes needed to create an environment in which the problem simply cannot exist. I call the method which can accomplish this the *Evaporating Clouds* method. Assuming that a core problem can be described as a big black cloud, then this method strives not to solve the problem (compromise) but to cause the problem not to exist.

whenever we face a situation which requires a compromise, there is always a simple solution that does not involve compromise.

The origin of the Evaporating Clouds method stems from the essence of two broadly accepted sentences. The first one, is more theological, "God does not limit us, we are limiting ourselves" and the second, which is regarded to be more practical, "You cannot have your cake and eat it too." These two sentences seem to be in contradiction. But the mere fact that they are so widely accepted indicates that both are valid. The second sentence is just a vivid description of the existence of compromising solutions. The first one probably indicates that, whenever we face a situation which requires a compromise, there is always a simple solution that does not involve compromise. We just have to find it.

How can we systematically find such solutions? Maybe the best place to start is by utilizing a third sentence, which is also very widely accepted: "define a problem precisely and you are halfway to a solution." Each one of us has most probably verified the validity of the last sentence more than once in our life.

Nevertheless there is one small difficulty, when do we usually realize the validity of the above sentence, only when we've already found the solution. Only then, in hindsight, do we recognize that the most decisive step in reaching a solution was actually the step where we precisely defined the problem. But how can we be sure that we have defined a problem precisely before having reached the solution?

Let's first examine what is the meaning of a problem. Intuitively we understand that a problem exists whenever there is something that prevents, or limits us, from reaching a desired objective. Therefore, defining a problem precisely must start with a declaration of the desired objective. What should we do next? Let's remind ourselves that what we are dealing with are the type of problems that involve compromise. A compromise between at least two bodies. In other words, we have to pacify, or satisfy, at least two different things if we want to achieve our desired objective.

"You can't have your cake and eat it too." From this analysis we can immediately conclude that whenever we are facing a problem which involves a compromise, there are at least two requirements which must be satisfied. In other words to reach the objective there are at least two necessary conditions which must be met. Thus, the next step in precisely defining a problem is to define the requirements that must be fulfilled. But the definition of the problem cannot stop here. We should realize that whenever a compromise exists, there must be at least one thing that is shared by the requirements and it is in this sharing that the problem, between the requirements, exists. Either we simply don't have enough to share or, in order to satisfy the requirements, we must do conflicting things, "you can't have your cake and eat it too." To put it more formally: to satisfy the requirements a prerequisite exists and it is here that the conflict arises—within the framework of the prerequisites.

Let's start by calling the desired objective "A." In order to reach "A" we must satisfy two different requirements, "B" and "C," where the prerequisite to satisfying "B" is "D" and the prerequisite to satisfying "C" is the opposite of "D." Or the prerequisite to satisfying "B" is some amount "D" that must be given to it and the prerequisite to satisfying "C" is some additional amount of "D" that must be given to it and we don't have enough of "D." A diagrammatic representation of this will look like:

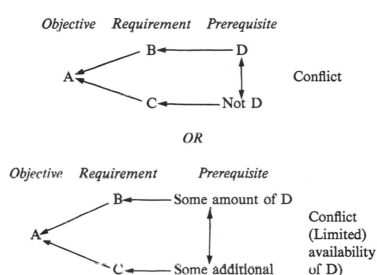

Even though the definition, of stating a problem precisely, looks logically sound, how can we substantiate it? Maybe the best way is to use the Effect-Cause-Effect method. The effect that we started with is "state a problem precisely and you're half way to solving it." The hypothesis is, the above diagrams are what is meant by stating a problem precisely. In order to verify this hypothesis, we must be able to explain, with the same hypothesis, an entirely different type of effect. Even though there are many such types of effects, I will bring into play here the effect that I originally used to verify this method.

At the time that the Evaporating Clouds method began to be formulated, I was deeply immersed in the field of scheduling and materials management. In that field there was one very awkward phenomena for which I couldn't find any logical explanation. One would expect that the articles published in professional magazines would deal with the problems that trouble the community of its readers. Therefore, one would expect that the bigger and more important the problem, the more articles there would be trying to address and solve that problem. Skimming the professional magazines in the field of materials management revealed a very awkward phenomena. In the last fifty years (actually from the thirties) the problem that attracted, by far the largest number of articles, is the problem of Economic Batch Quantity (EBQ). At the same time, talk to any practitioner and you'll find out that batch sizes are determined almost off the cuff and nobody in the plants is overly concerned about it. I don't think that it is an exaggeration to estimate that at least 10,000 articles have already been published on this subject. Certainly more than on the much more debatable subjects of scheduling, MRP or JIT. Why is this? What caused such a flood of articles into such a relatively unimportant problem?

What caused such a flood of articles into such a relatively unimportant problem? Maybe we can explain this phenomena, if what we find is that this particular problem had some unique feature. A feature that will attract the interests of those motivated by the academic measurement of "publish or perish." The only feature that could cause such an overabundance of articles, is that this problem of batch sizes, is a precisely defined problem. In such a case, people will certainly be more attracted to deal with a problem which is clearly defined, rather than with the more important problems which are vaguely stated. As it turns out this is exactly the case. The batch size problem is precisely defined, according to the above diagrams.

Let's review it in more detail, not to see what the batch size should be, but in order to acquire a much better understanding of the Evaporating Clouds method. The batch size problem is stated as: find the batch size that will result in the minimum cost per unit. The major avenues through which the size of the batch will impact the cost per unit are as follows.

1 The Setup Cost:

If we set up a machine for one hour and then produce only one unit of a given item, then this unit will have to carry the entire cost of the one hour of setup. But, if after the one hour setup, we produce ten units of a given item, then each unit will have to carry only one-tenth of the cost of one hour of setup.

Thus if we want to reduce the setup cost per unit, we should strive to produce in as large a batch as possible. Graphically the cost per unit as a function of batch size, when setup cost is considered, is shown in Figure 3.

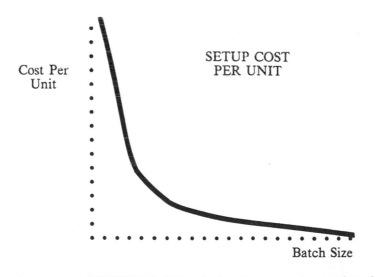

FIGURE 3: What is the cost per unit, as a function of batch size, when we consider the setup cost of our resources?

2 The Carrying Cost:

Setup is not the only channel by which the size of the batch impacts the cost per unit. We are all aware that as we enlarge the size of the batch we will enlarge the amount of time that we will hold the batch in our possession and thus we increase the carrying cost of inventory. Most articles indicate a linear relationship; doubling the size of the batch roughly doubles the carrying cost. When considering the carrying cost per unit, we should strive to produce in the smallest batches possible. Graphically the cost per unit as a function of batch size when carrying cost is considered is shown in Figure 4.

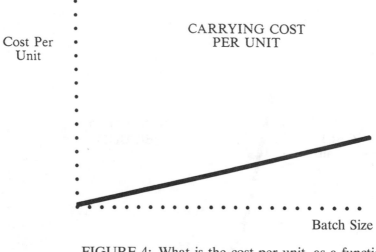

FIGURE 4: What is the cost per unit, as a function of batch size, when we consider the carrying cost? We are all aware that as we enlarge the batch we enlarge the time we hold it in our possession.

It is quite easy to see that the problem of batch size determination is actually a compromising problem which is precisely defined. The Evaporating Clouds diagram is quite evident:

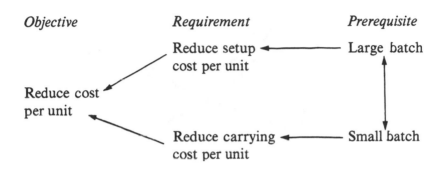

Objective   *Requirement*   *Prerequisite*

Reduce setup ◄─────────── Large batch
cost per unit

Reduce cost
per unit

Reduce carrying ◄─────────── Small batch
cost per unit

Actually, finding a solution is restricted by the question: what compromise should we make?

Now we should outline how to move systematically from defining the problem to finding a solution. But maybe it will behove us to first examine how such problems are treated conventionally. The conventional way is to accept the problem as a given and to search for a solution within the framework established by the problem. Thus, conventionally we concentrate on finding an "optimum" solution. Since we cannot satisfy both requirements, "B" and "C," all the efforts are aimed at finding out how much we can jeopardize each one, so that the damage to the objective "A" will be minimized. Actually, finding a solution is restricted by the question: what compromise should we make?

In the batch size problem, we consider the total cost, which is the summation of the setup and carrying cost contributions (see Figure 5). And then, we mathematically or numerically find the minimum cost possible, which indicates the "best" batch size.

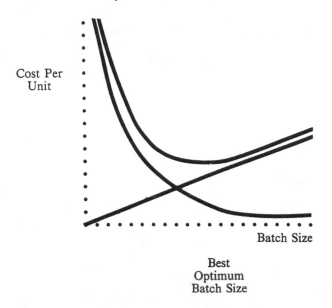

FIGURE 5: What is the cost per unit, as a function
of batch size, when we consider the
two major components (setup cost and
carrying cost) together?

This type of approach, with a whole variety of small corrective
considerations, is what appears in the vast number of articles
mentioned above. Most articles also point out that the curve is
very flat near the minimum and they claim that it's not too
terribly important which batch is chosen, as long as it is within
the range marked by the two circles in Figure 5. The intuitive,
off the cuff choice for a batch size that we make in reality, is
usually well within this range. This same point, about falling
within this wide range, is what made everyone wonder about the
practicality of all these academic articles, that while mentioning
it, are concentrating on small corrective factors that do not
change the picture in any significant way.

The Evaporating Clouds method does not strive to reach a
compromise solution, rather it concentrates on invalidating the
problem itself. The first attack is made on the objective itself
asking, "Do we really want it?" How can we find out? The easi-

est way is by comparing the objective in question to the global objective. This comparison is achieved by simply trying to re-state the problem using the terminology of the global objective rather than the local terminology.

Are we really trying to achieve a minimum cost per unit? Maybe, but what we are really trying to achieve is, of course, the making of more money. Since most readers have not yet devel-oped their intuition regarding Throughput, Inventory and Oper-ating Expense, we'll use, instead, the slightly more cumbersome global terminology of the relationships of making money; Net Profit and Return on Investment. Rather than using cost per unit, we should use profit per unit. Since, the problem assumes a fixed selling price; more cost less profit, less cost more profit, we can just replace cost by profit. This results in a mirror image of the previous graph (Figure 5).

How do we bring investment into the picture? We should just remind ourselves of the reason for the linear relationship (straight line) between carrying cost and the batch size. Dou-bling the batch size means doubling the carrying cost. But this implies doubling the investment in the work in process and fin-ished goods material that we hold. In other words, there is also a linear relationship between the batch size and investment. Thus, we can simply replace the horizontal axis (batch size) with in-vestment (in WIP and FG's) and we get a graph which is profit per unit versus investment, as shown in Figure 6.

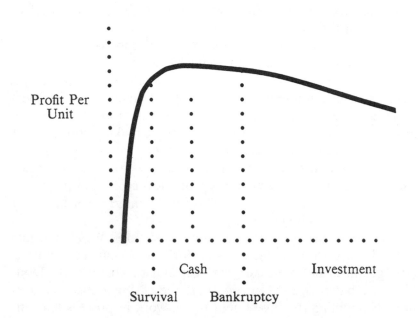

FIGURE 6: When we consider a fixed selling price
             for our products and inventory as an in-
             vestment, the mirror image of cost per
             unit versus batch size becomes profit
             per unit versus investment.

All the batches within the two circles provide about the same
profit or, as before, about the same cost. But what about return
on investment? The same profit means the same return, but the
investment in that interval has more than doubled. If we want to
make more money, then we shouldn't aim for the top of the
curve but at some point substantially to the left of it. And what
about that brutal, necessary condition called cash?

Suppose that the plant has an amount of cash which resides
somewhere between the two points (as indicated by the bar on
the investment axis). Do you still regard the two circles as equiv-

alent points? Yes, they are equivalent from the point of view of the net profit, but in this case one means bankruptcy and the other survival.

Almost no one bothers to check the local objectives versus the global goal.

This "optimal" solution has been taught for more than 50 years in almost every university around the globe. Almost no one bothers to check the local objectives versus the global goal. Let's not fool ourselves, this phenomena is not restricted to just academic problems but is widespread in real life. How many times has your company worked so hard to win a bid and once it was won, it turned out to be a disaster? How many times have you seen a foreman forced to break setups, go to overtime, in order to expedite some pieces, just to find them two weeks later gathering dust in a warehouse? How many times have you almost climbed the walls to meet tolerances that shouldn't have been there in the first place? Our experience shows that over 90% of the problems that industrial organizations are struggling with, on a day to day basis, belong to exactly that category of problems. Problems that arise whenever we try to satisfy local objectives that do not match, at all, the global goal.

behind any logical connection there is an assumption. In our case, most probably it is a hidden assumption.

Coming back to the method of Evaporating Clouds, let's assume for now that the objective has been checked and verified. Yes, we do want to achieve this specific objective. Is the only way open to turn to the avenue of compromise? The answer is definitely not. What we have to remind ourselves of, is that the arrows in the Evaporating Clouds diagram, the arrows connecting the requirements to the objective, the pre-requisite to the requirements and the arrow of the conflict, all these arrows are just logical connections. One of the most basic fundamentals of logic is, that behind any logical connection there is an assumption. In our case, most probably it is a hidden assumption.

Let's clarify it with an example taken from the *Theory of Constraints Journal.** Suppose that the objective "A" is to "reach the top of Mount Everest." Why? It doesn't matter, "because it's there." Requirement "B" appears in our diagram (which revolves around insufficient money) as: "participants must be expert mountain climbers." It looks logical but the connection between "B" and "A" is based on an unstated assumption. The assumption that we intend to reach the top of Mount Everest by climbing. It is enough just to verbalize this assumption and pictures of parachutes and helicopters start to flash in our minds.

The Evaporating Clouds technique is based on verbalizing the assumptions hidden behind the arrows, forcing them out and challenging them. It's enough to invalidate even one of these assumptions, no matter which one, and the problem collapses, disappears. The previous Mount Everest example probably left you with a sour taste in your mouth, as it is too simplistic, unfair.

So maybe we should try to use this technique on the batch size problem. Let's remember that this problem is one in which more than 10,000 bright people have invested so much time trying to solve (to the extent that they have published articles about it). Evaporating this problem certainly serves, in more than one way, as a good illustration of the validity of the Evaporating Clouds method.

Examine, for example, the arrow connecting requirement "B" to the objective. The influence of setup cost on cost per unit is the unstated assumption that was taken when we drew the batch size problem. It doesn't take long to realize that we have taken setup as a given. In other words, we assumed that the setup cost is fixed and cannot be reduced. What do we call the method that so viciously attacks this assumption? We call it JIT. JIT has proven that just the realization (that setup is not fixed) is almost enough to enable us to achieve (in a relatively small period of

* Volume 1, Number 2, Article 1.

time and with relative small investment) drastic reductions in setup. Sometimes from many hours to just a few minutes.

But there are many ways to have our cake and eat it to. So, let's try to find out if there is another assumption hiding behind the same arrow. Just thinking about it probably sends flickers through your mind: "does setup really cost us money?" Before you dismiss this, why don't you try to phrase this same thought using the Theory of Constraints terminology. Remember, the Theory of Constraints shies away from the word *cost,* like it was fire.

But the word cost is also used in a third way, that of "product cost," which is just an artificial, mathematical phantom.

The word cost belongs to the most dangerous and confusing category of words—the multi-meaning words. We use this word as a synonym for purchase price, like in the sentence, "the cost of a machine." We use it as a synonym for Operating Expense, like in the sentence, "the cost to run the operation." This means that by using the word cost we might confuse investment (the first meaning) with expense (the second meaning). You might become rich by prudent investments but certainly not by spending your money. But the word cost is also used in a third way, that of "product cost," which is just an artificial, mathematical phantom (*Theory of Constraints Journal,* Volume 1, Number 4, Article 1).

After this long remark on the multiple meanings of the word cost, let's try to rephrase the question ("does setup really cost us money?") this time using the term Operating Expense. The lightbulb just went on. The equivalent is "will an additional setup increase the Operating Expense of the organization?" Rather than putting it aside, with a smiling no, let's investigate it in more depth.

Suppose that all the people who have tried to solve the batch size problem would have dealt with a situation, where at least one of the resources involved in the setup was a bottleneck. This certainly cannot be the case, since in such a situation, the impact of doing an additional setup would not be an increase in Operating Expense but rather a much more devastating impact, a decrease in Throughput. So let's assume that the situation they have dealt with, is one in which none of the resources involved in the setup is a bottleneck. In such a case the impact of doing an additional setup on Operating Expense is basically zero.

What we see is that exposing the hidden assumption is sufficient for us to understand that the whole problem revolved around a distortion in terminology. What is our answer to the batch size now? Where should we have large batches? On the bottlenecks and everywhere else? Let's have smaller batches. Small, to the extent that we can afford the additional setups, without turning the other resources into bottlenecks.

What I would like to demonstrate is that every arrow can be challenged. But since I don't want to turn this into the 10,001 book on batch sizes, let me demonstrate it by concentrating on what is perceived to be the most solid arrow in the diagram— the arrow of the conflict itself. What is the assumption behind "large batch is the opposite of small batch"? That large is the opposite of small? To challenge this means to challenge mathematics itself. So the only avenue left open is to challenge the assumption, that the word *batch* does not belong to that category of words having multiple meanings. Here, it seems that we are at a loss, where the only way out is to ask ourselves if we know of any environment, in which the concept of batch does not fit. Yes, we all know of such environments—flow lines, continuous production, assembly lines. It seems to reason that batch sizing is not applicable in such environments, because in those environments the distinction between the two meanings of the word batch is so big that we cannot possibly group them together.

What is the batch size in a dedicated assembly line, dedicated to the assembly of one type of product? Of course it's one; we are moving the products along the assembly line in batches of one. But on second thought, another answer is there as well. How many units do we process one after the other, before we stop and reset the line to assemble another type of product? A very large number, we don't ever reset a dedicated line.

What are we going to do now? It seems as if we have two correct answers to the same question, where the first answer is one and the second is infinite. Rather then putting the whole thing aside, by saying that the batch size concept is not applicable to such situations, let's try to verbalize the lessons that we can extract from it. We reached the answer one, when we looked on this situation from the point of view of the product. The unverbalized question was actually, "how many units do we batch together for the purpose of transferring them, from one resource to another along the line?" The answer one was thus given, in order to describe the size of the batch used for the purpose of transferring the units through the resources—we call it the *transfer-batch*. On the other hand, we reached the answer of infinite from the point of view of the resources in the line. The question here was "how many units do we batch together for the purpose of processing them, one after the other"? The answer infinite was thus given to describe the size of the batch used for the purpose of processing—we call it the *process batch*.

In every flow environment, we find very strong indications that the process batch and the transfer batch are totally different entities that can and do co-exist, even when we consider the same items, on the same resource, at the same time. We move batches of one through a machine on the line, while at the same time the process batch, in which these parts are processed by the machine, is infinite.

Now let's return to our problem: why did we have the prerequisite of a large batch? To save setup. In other words, the batch that we wanted to be large, was the process batch. Why did we have the pre-requisite of a small batch? Because we wanted to reduce the carrying cost of inventory—the time that we hold the inventory in our possession. In other words, we wanted a small transfer batch. Why then do we claim that we have a conflict, when these two pre-requisites can be fully satisfied, at the same time.

The entire problem that bothered so many people for more than 50 years was due to the improper use of terminology.

The entire problem that bothered so many people for more than 50 years was due to the improper use of terminology. Now the solution is obvious. We should strive to maximize the process batches on the bottlenecks, while at the same time using small transfer batches everywhere—including through the bottleneck (small transfer batches do not have any impact on setup). The efforts to find the "best" batch size, should have been directed towards straightening out the paper work on the shop floor rather than finding some artificial optimum. Otherwise, "work-orders" will arbitrarily force the transfer batch to be equal to the process batch.

Read *The Goal,* if you have already read it read it again, and whenever you find Alex developing a simple, common sense solution, that's exactly where the Evaporating Clouds method was used. *The Race,* which is devoted to explaining why inventory is even more important than operating expenses, is actually a collection of examples that make extensive use of the Effect-Cause-Effect and Evaporating Clouds methods. Here, for example, is an arbitrary page from *The Race.* Try to reconstruct the Effect-Cause-Effect tree and the Evaporating Clouds diagram that lead to the conclusions outline on these pages.

An Excerpt From:

THE RACE

LOW INVENTORY—THE KEY TO MORE ACCURATE FORECASTS

In order to understand the impact of work-in-process inventory on due dates we must examine something that looks at first glance as totally unrelated—the validity of our product forecast.

Almost every plant has a forecast of demand which is quite reliable for some period of time into the future, then the validity of the forecast drastically deteriorates within a very short period of time. What causes this universal phenomenon?

If all companies in an industry are providing delivery of a product within two months, then customers will not place orders and commit themselves to specific due dates a year in advance. They probably will place their orders about 2½ months before they need the product. Even when they place an order for a whole year, they will feel free to change the quantity and ship date two months in advance without risk of jeopardizing deliveries or placing their vendors in an impossible situation. Consequently, the plant's forecast for this product will be quite reliable for the first two months and quite unreliable for the period beyond three months. If we operate with high inventory relative to our competitors, it means that our production lead time is longer than the valid forecast horizon of the industry. The length of the valid horizon will be dictated by our low inventory competitors. As a result, the high inventory company's production plans are based on pure guesses and not on a reliable forecast.

It's no wonder that due-date performance is a problem where we have high inventories. When we operate in a lower inventory mode than our competitors, we enjoy an enviable position that gives us an inherently more accurate forecast. Now when we start production, we have firm orders or a valid forecast which is much less likely to change. Our due-date performance will certainly be much improved. Our production plans are now driven by more reliable information and we are in a much better position to give reliable requirements to our vendors. Remember, a prime reason that our vendors cannot deliver reliably is because we keep changing our requirements on them, the same way our customers are changing their requirements on us.

How about the last competitive element, shorter quoted lead times? We will again find that inventory plays an unexpected role?

HIGH VS. LOW INVENTORY SYSTEMS:
DUE DATE PERFORMANCE

High Inventory   *Low Inventory*

High Inventory   **Low Inventory**

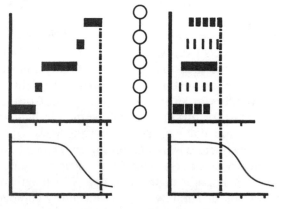

FORECAST VALIDITY

FORECAST VALIDITY

Production starts   Production starts
based on a guess.   based on good
We oscillate   knowledge. Due
between excess   date performance
finished goods,   < < 90%.
inventory and
missed due dates.

In order to demonstrate that both *The Goal* and *The Race* cover only a small portion of the applications of the Theory of Constraints, even as far as production itself is concerned, the next example, I would like to present, is from the *Theory of Constraints Journal.** This article is an excellent demonstration of the use of the Effect-Cause-Effect method in pinpointing core problems (notice that Jonah insists on diving

* Volume 1, Number 3, Article 2.

three levels deep in the logical tree) and the Evaporating Clouds method is used to highlight simple solutions. But not less important is how these methods merge together to enable the effective use of the Socratic method.

An excerpt from:

The Theory of Constraints Journal
Volume 1, Number 3, Article 2

A VISIT
When Quoted Lead Times Are The Problem

"In manufacturing we have people who are getting much better at dealing with their constraints. Al has done a lot of work. Tom, one of our plant managers has made some physical changes on the floor that really made a nice, big difference. More than once we have broken bottlenecks and now we can ship things we were not going to ship before." Bert—the company's president—takes a deep breath and turning to Chris, his V.P. of Operations, remarks, "We have quite a few Alex Rogo's in your area. In my opinion the problem is no longer in manufacturing!"

Chris, leaning back in his chair answers slowly, not looking at anybody in particular, as if voicing his internal thoughts. "At this stage I would say that we don't have any more bottlenecks—we broke them all. I would estimate that we have cut our work-in-process inventory to about one half of its historical level. But in the last six months we haven't reduced it by more than 10%, maybe 20% at the most. I'm afraid that we are once again stagnating."

It's a little bit unusual. To visit a company that achieves a 50% reduction in work-in-process, and still pushes forward, is not so surprising. But to call an additional 10% improvement, stagnation—that is unusual. Accurate but not unusual.

"I can't agree that we should be satisfied with the current performance of manufacturing." Chris continues. "For example, the gap between our computer systems and the reality on the shop floor is widening. Al, can't you do something about it?"

"Come on, Chris," Al the Director of Materials replies, "the situation is not so bad. My people do release all material's schedule promptly. What can I do if sometimes we have to release partial orders because Engineering slips their schedule? Overall, I don't think that our systems are much worse than the rest of our industry. The accuracy of our data is quite good, even though I would like to get a little bit more cooperation from your production people in this area. You must admit that the timeliness of reporting transactions on the floor can be substantially improved."

"Al, we have discussed it more than once," Chris sighs. "How can we insist on prompt reporting of each transaction, when the updated report is available only once a week? The superintendents and foremen are already complaining that the hassle to feed the computer is too much. If you want better and faster data from the floor, you need to provide updated feedback reports within a day, not a week."

"Our system simply can't do it. The computer is so loaded that it's a miracle that you get the response we are currently giving. You know that almost every weekend my people have to stay to guarantee that everything will be ready on Monday morning. If you need faster response, and I agree on that point one hundred percent, we must go to an online system." Al shifts his eyes to Bert. "That means a new, larger, computer and a new state-of-the-art system."

Bert is not impressed at all. "I know that we can pour more money into computers, but the fact is that manufacturing has improved dramatically without investing anything in computers. No, I maintain that the problem is no longer in production. It is on the preparation side of the house. J.P., your area must improve!"

"I know that we can pour more money into computers, but the fact is that manufacturing has improved dramatically without investing anything in computers."

This company is in the business of bidding on furnishing new facilities, such as supplying the furniture for a new laboratory or an auditorium. In this business everything is made to order and the engineering and paperwork functions needed to design and specify the furniture are a big part of the organization. J.P. is in charge of the "preparation" activities and it's apparent that he has been under the gun for quite some time.

"Bert, I don't have to tell you that preparing the drawings is not a trivial task. We must have more modern technology if we want to change things around here. Our CAD systems are simply not good enough. We must provide our people with new systems. I gave you my estimates of the cost involved. It will take us quite some time to train our people properly to use these new systems. Every postponement in the decision just delays further when we can improve. If you decide today, we can improve our side by more than 30% in less than 12 months. I know that the payback is a little bit more than two years, but if we have to do it, let's do it."

"More computers, more technology, more investments, that cannot be the only answer!" Bert starts to explode. "The technology we use today is infinitely better than what we used even ten years ago, but I haven't noticed a comparable improvement in the results. I doubt if today we are responding much faster than ten years ago."

"The bids are much more complicated," J.P. murmurs under his breath.

Chris and Al nod their heads in approval.

"I'm not so convinced," Bert replies. And then turning to me he says, "You see Jonah, it seems that we cannot even agree on where our constraints are."

I shift uneasily in my chair. It's quite tempting to agree with Bert and to dive into the subject matter, to try and sort out the maze. But it's obvious that this conversation, or a variation of it, has taken place more than once in the past. Thus, it seems reasonable to expect that an intuitive, underlying agreement of the problem, has already been very well established. The best way to proceed is to expose this unverbalized agreement.

"No Bert, I cannot say that I see it," I start. "To tell the truth, I have the feeling of someone who enters a movie an hour after it has started. I'm still trying to figure out what's going on. Somehow I have the impression that while you don't agree on the tactics, at the same time, the strategy is agreed on to the extent that you already take it for granted."

They all smile and Chris says, "It's very comfortable to hear that we all agree on something, but unfortunately I don't think that your impression is correct."

I wait for the laughs to calm down and facing Bert, I ask, "What is the biggest business problem facing your company now?"

Bert answers immediately, "We don't win enough bids."

J.P. nods and adds, "Competition is more fierce than ever."

I shift my eyes to Chris and in reply he says, "No doubt. As I said, we have broken all our bottlenecks in production. We can easily handle more orders." After a short while a broad smile spreads across his face and winking his right eye he says, "We do agree on something. You are right. We do agree on the most important thing—on our biggest business problem."

The tension has left the room. I puff on my cigar waiting for Bert to pick up the conversation, which he does. "Touche. But this agreement doesn't preclude us from violently disagreeing on where the constraint is now."

I don't answer, but it doesn't take long until J.P. supplies the answer. "But we do agree on the major constraint. We just said that our current major constraint is the market."

"Yes, of course," says Bert impatiently. "What we actually don't agree on, is how to elevate it."

A hum of agreement is in the room.

> *Leaving things at the intuition level makes communication almost impossible.*

Verbalizing what we know intuitively, is a foundation on which we can build our next steps. Leaving things at the intuition level makes communication almost impossible. Thus when a team effort to find a solution is made, it is almost essential not to leave important steps unverbalized. I'm trying to be very careful not to fall into that trap myself. In the conversation they didn't even speculate about the reasons for insufficient sales, indicating that that is another thing that is totally agreed upon among them.

"I have the impression that you agree on an additional thing," I say. "What is the major stumbling block to getting more sales? Is it price, quality or something else?"

Bert answers confidently— "It's not price or quality. It is certainly our too long quoted delivery lead times. You see Jonah, our clients are almost always pressed for time. Maybe it's because furnishing a new facility is the last step in completing it. So if we quote 20 weeks from receipt of order until everything is mounted at the client site, it's always too long. And if a competitor is quoting 10 weeks, he will get the order. Yes, there is a lot of cheating going around, but I insist on quoting reliable estimates. As a matter of fact, we have a very good reputation for delivering when promised. We get quite a few orders because of our reputation. Many times, when a competitor slips significantly on his promised date, the order is transferred to us. No, I will not allow false quotes."

"Nevertheless many times we have to climb up the walls to meet the promise date," Al throws a remark into the room.

"That's the understatement of the year," Chris adds with a tortured expression on his face.

"Yes, this is a fair assessment. Our prices are good. We have very high quality products. We have good designs. The problem is definitely in our long quoted lead times. In many cases, too many cases, the competition is quoting as low as half the time. To reduce our estimates, is to squeeze the system even more and you see it's impossible. It's already tight as it is. We must use better and faster technology if we want to reduce the quoted times and still be reliable."

"Here we go again," says Bert.

I do a quick assessment in my mind. The core of the disagreement between Bert and J.P. is quite obvious. They simply differ in their basic assumptions. J.P.'s assumption is that if his people will do their jobs more quickly, the company will be able to quote shorter lead times. Bert's intuition leads him to assume that the current long quoted lead times are unrelated to the speed at which each individual job is done, but related to the synchronization between the jobs.

He had already proven to himself that drastic lead time reduction can be achieved without improving the individual processes.

Chris' disagreement must stem from a different source. He had already proven to himself that drastic lead time reduction can be achieved without improving the individual processes. What is it? Can it be that manufacturing is still the biggest contributor to lead time or is it just part of the political power struggle? Something does not click since Chris didn't ask for any new investments. And what about Chris' remark on the widening gap between the floor and the computer system? Al succeeded, probably unintentionally, in diverting him, but something important must lie under Chris' remark. I've too much respect for management intuition to ignore it. Questions! Questions!

How to peer into it? I decide to continue in the most obvious way. If they claim that their quoted lead times are the major cause of their marketing constraint, let's dig into this subject.

"Bert, you all say that the long quote lead times preclude you from winning enough bids. Can you give me a rough breakdown of the components of this lead time? What are the activities, and estimates of their duration, that you take into account before quoting a delivery date to a prospect?"

"It differs from bid to bid," Bert starts slowly, searching for a way to clarify this complex situation to an outsider who does not "live" his business. "There are very small orders and also very large and complicated bids. Let's take, for example, an average bid, something in the range of $100 to $300 thousand. A typical breakdown will be something like four weeks for the design, then there's approval . . . J.P. this is your area. Can you help me?"

"Certainly," J.P. says. "As a matter of fact I have some statistics here on the various bids. You wanted bids between $100 and $300 thousand . . . just a minute." Quickly he sifts through a pile of papers that he has brought with him. After a very short while he raises his head. "Here is a breakdown of quotes for laboratories in the range of $100 to $250 thousand. It takes one week to process the order, five weeks to draw the project, two weeks to approve the drawings with the customer, one week to enter the corrections to the drawings and then two weeks to prepare it for release to manufacturing. Then add ten weeks for manufacturing plus one week in shipping and five weeks for installation."

"Thank you," says Bert and turning to me he continues, "add it all up and you get . . . 26 weeks. The competition is quoting about 20 weeks, which means that we promise to ship our first truck when our competitor is promising to complete the entire order. When the client is pressed for time, we can even offer it for free and it will not help us to get the order."

I nod my head to indicate that the severity of the problem is well understood, waiting for Chris to jump in, which he doesn't. That puzzles me. The numbers certainly support Chris' position that manufacturing is still the major area to focus on. From the 26 weeks quoted, 16 weeks are needed after all the preparation is completed. Why doesn't Chris take this opportunity to clearly demonstrate his point?

"When the client is pressed for time, we can even offer it for free and it will not help us to get the order."

Conversation has stopped and everybody is looking at me. Maybe on-site construction, or as they call it 'installation,' does not report to Chris. If this is the case, then he is responsible for just 10 weeks out of the 26. This seems a remote possibility since Chris' title, "Vice President of Operations" indicates that he is responsible for more than just manufacturing. Besides, if another person was responsible for installation, it is reasonable to expect that Bert would have invited him to this meeting. Since I cannot find any other plausible explanation, I turn to Chris. "Who is responsible for the one-site-construction?" I ask.

"Me," comes the answer.

each person, when asked to evaluate the time it will take to complete a task, will instinctively add a safety factor.

Now what? I wonder. Can it be that Chris does not believe in these numbers and thus hesitates to use them as a base for his position? This might be the answer. Certainly there is not a direct communication between Chris' production people and the people who prepare the quotes for the bids. They report to J.P. From my experience I've learned that each person, when asked to evaluate the time it will take to complete a task, will instinctively add a safety factor. If the process involves a series of people, each will add an additional safety and the end result will be vastly exaggerated. This phenomena takes on grotesque proportions when the people in marketing and product engineering don't exactly trust the production people, and thus will tend to protect themselves, against future complaints from clients, by inflating the time estimates.

So it is reasonable to assume that Chris does not agree at all with the numbers that J.P. has quoted. But how to verify it? I cannot take a straightforward approach and simply ask Chris if he does not agree with the numbers. At Chris' and J.P.'s levels, they are very careful not to get into an open confrontation in front of their boss. A direct question will just put Chris in a very embarrassing situation and the only thing that will result, is a very vague "political" statement.

If my hypothesis is right, the recent reduction in production lead time, will not be fully reflected in the estimates currently used in the quotations. The same overprotective mechanism will guarantee it. The next (now) obvious question is, "What did you use as an estimate for the production lead time of such an order two years ago?"

"About 12 weeks," J. P. answers.

Bingo! The quoted production lead times have gone down by only 2 weeks even though the actual production lead time dropped by much more. I make a fast calculation in my head. The work-in-process inventories were cut by more than 50%. The level of work-in-process is proportional to production lead times (see *The Race* pages 64–65). The current production lead time is probably less than 6 weeks, not 10 weeks.

The dichotomy does not escape Bert. "Wait a minute," he says, "the actual reduction in manufacturing is much more than two weeks. Chris, what is your estimate?"

"I would say that in the last year, manufacturing has cut at least five weeks," Chris replies. "Everybody knows that we have made major strides in this area."

J.P. raises his hand. "Sorry fellows. My people must rely on the numbers that are supplied by the computer. According to what is reported, the production lead time has dropped by only two weeks."

In response Chris immediately turns to Al. "You see what happens when we have such a crooked production planning system? I've told you a hundred times that the gap between our computer system and the reality on the floor is intolerable!"

Al looks totally puzzled. "But these numbers don't have anything to do with the production planning system. They are derived directly from the completion dates reported by the production people. It is impossible that such a gross error is generated by the computer."

It's a fact," Chris states, but even he looks unconvinced.

"I don't care what the damn computer says," Bert cuts into the argument. "Everybody knows that the production lead time has been cut by more than just two weeks. J.P., your people must update their numbers. It's essential. This overcaution is costing us the entire business."

J.P. doesn't look too enthusiastic.

"The minute that we start to ignore hard numbers and start to rely on things that everybody knows, there is no way to predict where it will end. Bert, I agree that something is wrong, and maybe very wrong. But the fact is that the hard numbers indicate only two weeks reduction and even now we sometimes have difficulties completing an installation on time."

He has a point, but I'm totally unsatisfied with the president's response.

"J.P., it is still obvious that something is wrong. Will you please look into it in depth?" Bert presses.

"Yes, of course," is the expected answer, but it's apparent that nothing will actually be done.

• • •

"Do you have difficulties in completing every order?" I ask Chris.

"No, no," he replies. "Lately we finish some orders even ahead of the promised date and most are met without exceptional hassle. But those that we have difficulties with are enough to make you old."

"What percentage of the orders do you have difficulties with?"

"I would estimate that about 80% of top management is absorbed in fire fighting."

"Oh, not many, thank God. But there is always at least one. And they are draining everybody's time. For example, just now, we have a serious emergency. It's a last minute change that has caused us to work overtime in one of our shops, for the last two days. A special truck delivery had to be arranged and the entire construction schedule is disrupted. I envision that I'll probably have to go to the site personally, to straighten things out." "It's constant fire fighting," Bert contributes his share. "I would estimate that about 80% of top management time is absorbed in fire fighting."

Everybody nods his head in full agreement.

"You mentioned that the current problem order was due to a last minute change," I ask.

"Which the client has handsomely paid for," J.P. remarks.

"Yes, I assume so," I continue. "Would you say, Chris, that last minute changes are the cause for the vast majority of these problem orders?"

"Yes, definitely," Chris answers in a very confident tone. "If it wasn't for these last minute changes, and sometimes the changes come after the last minute, there is no problem at all. I can categorically state that in the last year we haven't had any problems with any order that didn't involve last minute changes."

A very thoughtful expression is now on Bert's face. After a short while he turns to J.P.

"The clients are paying very handsomely for these changes. I wonder if it is really the case."

"We are charging more than twice the usual rate for changes. If that is not a nice price, what is?"

"but if these are the things that absorb most of management's time, I wonder if it pays."

"Yes, we charge twice as much," Bert continues in a thoughtful tone, "but if these are the things that absorb most of management's time, I wonder if it pays." After a short while he continues, "And if due to these changes, we are under the impression that our lead time estimates are not conservative enough . . . I wonder how many bids we have lost due to this probably false impression."

"Even if we want to stop it, we can't," J.P., reading what Bert is alluding to, hurries to state. "We cannot stop a client from making changes and we simply cannot charge more without creating an outrage. As long as the client doesn't feel that it is absolutely too late, he feels free to make changes. And we, as a reputable company, must respond."

"Yes, I see what you mean," sighs Bert.

After a short while I ask, "What do you think makes a client feel that it is too late?"

Everyone looks at me as if I have asked an improper question. But J.P. answers, "When it's obvious that it's too late."

I feel a little bit stupid, but I keep on looking steadily at J.P. until he adds, "Like when all the pieces are already on the client's site and construction has started."

"Hey, that is not necessarily the case," Chris jumps in. "Take, for example, this current problem order. We definitely received the change after the last truck was sent."

"It might be the case. But most probably the client initiated the change at least two weeks before," J.P. answers.

"So, as our quoted lead times are longer, we simply give more time for the client to change his mind."

"I see," says Bert. "So, as our quoted lead times are longer, we simply give more time for the client to change his mind. Which causes last minute changes. Which gives us the impression that our quoted lead times are not long enough. Which prevents us from cutting them, even if the reality is that our production lead time has been shortened dramatically. How did we allow such a vicious cycle?"

"Come to think about it," Al adds oil to the fire, "in all cases where we are not hit by last minute surprises, the actual construction is finished well ahead of time."

"Yes," Chris contributes his share. "The big allowance for construction time was never due to the actual time of construction, but in order to enable us to ship the last pieces that were always missing. After we broke all our bottlenecks this situation improved dramatically."

"What is your estimate for construction time?" Bert asks.

"For the type of bid that we are discussing, it certainly is below three weeks," Chris replies.

"That's my impression," is Al's back up.

"So I see," Bert speaks, looking at nobody in particular. "We exaggerate our production estimates by about 4 weeks and then two more weeks in construction. Here are the six weeks we are missing."

He looks at J.P.

But before Bert can summarize, J.P. jumps in. "We should

check this new assumption about the shrinkage of construction time." He emphasizes the words "new assumption" to the extent that it's clear that his opinion on this subject is vastly different. "I believe it's possible to separate the orders that do not contain any last minute changes, and then check the reported construction time. If there are no unforeseen problems, I think that we can dig out the facts in less than one month."

"I don't see why we have to wait a month for something that we already know," Bert starts to lose his patience. "This business has started to lose money because we don't win enough bids. The times that we could afford this overcaution are over. We must move and move fast. J.P. I don't want any postponement in the implementation of what we just found. The lead times, quoted in the bids, must be cut immediately."

"If that's what you want," comes the very reluctant answer.

Bert is not too happy with J.P.'s response and so, after a short silence, he continues, "Competition is more fierce than ever, those were your words, J.P. We must move aggressively in order to keep pace. I'm sure that you understand. Sometimes we have to take chances."

It is quite obvious that he feels good. I don't.

"As long as we all understand that it is taking a chance," J.P. says. "Yes, I understand your decision and you can count on me to take all the necessary steps immediately."

"Thank you," says Bert. He looks around with a determined expression on his face.

It is quite obvious that he feels good. I don't.

• • •

The three of them are chatting about something, using the local jargon that is characteristic of each plant, so I stand up to pour myself a cup of coffee. I wonder why it is that we are so satisfied with finding solutions for immediate problems and are so reluctant to expose the causes. It's not the first time that I've witnessed it, and unfortunately, it won't be the last time.

Bert stands up and joins me.

"Jonah, you don't look very happy. What's the matter?"

"Jonah, you don't look very happy. What's the matter? Aren't you satisfied with what we achieved this morning?"

"Oh yes," I answer. "But we cannot ignore the fact that some questions have been left unanswered."

"Which questions?" asks Bert, certainly interested.

"There are several. For example, why do the numbers indicate that production lead times have been reduced by just two weeks?"

"Hey, that's computer stuff. I'm certain that the reduction is at least five weeks. Probably more."

It's clear that in his mind this problem is a triviality. "And Chris' complaint about the widening gap between systems and the shop floor?" I continue.

"Jonah, don't worry. It's just the same computer stuff," Bert answers confidently.

"Maybe," I say, "Nevertheless, passing on erroneous information might be hazardous."

"Yes, I agree," says Bert, but he doesn't seem to be too concerned. "Any other open questions?" he asks.

"Nothing, except for clarifying the root cause for the disagreements among you."

"What disagreements?" he asks in a much more interested tone.

"If I'm not mistaken, you claimed this morning that the problems have shifted to the preparation side of the house. We didn't touch on this subject at all."

"Yes, that's true."

"And besides, J.P. and Al are quite convinced that they can improve only if additional investments are approved. Let's remember that even if this reduction in the quoted lead times can be implemented without problems, it will just put you on par with your competitor. I assume that they will continue to improve their performance and thus you still have to face this demand for more investments."

"You are absolutely right, Jonah," he says. "Why don't we return to the table and continue our discussion."

I pour myself another cup and we all sit down.

"Al, can I ask you some technical questions," I start. "How do you plan the material release?"

"We have an MRP computer system. We bought a commercial package and modified it considerably to fit our particular needs."

"Can you be a little bit more specific?" I slowly light my cigar to indicate that we have all the time in the world.

"We have an MRP computer system. We bought a commercial package and modified it considerably to fit our particular needs."

"It's actually very simple," Al continues, "as long as we don't dive into the tiny, nitty gritty, of course. Once the information is coded by J.P.'s people, you know the bill of materials and the routings, we explode down the requirements from the specified shipping dates. Our bill of material is quite deep. It ranges from 6 to up to 11 levels, so we net the requirements against the stocks at each level and . . ."

I raise my eyebrows in surprise. I was under the impression that they build just to order, so what stocks is he talking about?

Al, noticing my surprise, hurries to clarify the issue. "There are many standard finished products and certainly many standard components. These we manufacture to forecast. So there is a need to net at each level. Besides at almost every level we use standard purchased components that we hold in stock."

"What are the lead times you are using in your MRP data base?" I ask.

"The usual. One week for each level," comes the reply.

"Bert, who looked somewhat bored during the discussion of these technical details, cannot hold back his surprise.

"What? A week for each stage of assembly? Have I heard you right?"

Chris comes to Al's aid. "It's not intended to reflect the actual assembly time, Bert. It's the traditional number that we have used for years to allow all the components to be gathered together. You know the problem of assembly. All fifty parts that are needed to be assembled are there, except for one."

"Oh," says Bert. "But if we take a week for each level, how did you actually reduce your work-in-progress?"

"We don't release to the floor according to the timing of the computer. We just use the quantities it specifies," Chris answers with a broad smile. And, turning to me he continues, "We have learned something from *The Goal*. We are using the painting area as the 'Herbie'. It's not a real bottleneck any more, we have improved it so much, that we operate it only 2 shifts 5 days a week, instead of running constantly on weekends, as in the past. But at our current level of manning, it's definitely a 'Herbie'."

"But if we take a week for each level, how did you actually reduce your work-in-process?"

Turning back to Bert he continues, "Today my superintendents delay the release of material by more than a month and time the release according to the rate of the paint shop. It's working very well. It also gives us a nice protection against delays in the release of the last drawing for an order. It was a big problem before."

"Yes, I've noticed that you don't complain about it any more," says Bert.

It's obvious that he is deep in thought. You can almost hear the wheels clicking in his head.

After a short while he continues, "so that is the reason why J.P.'s numbers indicated that the production lead times have been reduced by only two weeks. Most of the lead time reduction was used to increase the time gap between preparation and manufacturing, rather than reduce the delivery time." He pauses and then slowly he asks, "Chris, to time the release of all the work must be a lot of manual effort. How do you handle it?"

"That is exactly what I'm complaining about. We have to work with old computer lists and spend a great deal of time basically monitoring everything manually," Chris replies in a voice that indicates, "at last somebody understands."

Bert turns to face Al. "Why shouldn't the computer do these calculations?"

Al, with a miserable expression on his face answers, "I've explained it to Chris more than once. Our systems simply are not capable of doing it."

"And the new online systems that you are so inclined to purchase. Can they do it?" presses Bert.

Now Al looks really miserable, and with a twisted grin he says, "I really didn't check into it thoroughly, because I actually don't know what to check. But I suspect that they are not much different than what we already have, except for speed and online capabilities, of course."

> *"So, we will be able to make the same mistakes faster and on a bigger scale."*

"So, we will be able to make the same mistakes faster and on a bigger scale," Bert concludes sardonically. After a minute or two Bert starts again. "We must do something about it. We can't leave all the benefit of the lead time improvement in manufacturing, it's on the wrong side of the process. We must use it to shorten the overall lead time, rather than just to increase the protection between preparation and production. Jonah, can you help me?"

I puff on my cigar for a short while and then say, "You don't need me to tell you the answer. Your people know how to do it."

"But we don't," says Al almost desperately.

"Al," I say. "Am I right in assuming that your people are doing this manual work for the production superintendents?"

"Yes, you are right," answers Chris instead. "The cooperation between the production and the material people is very good."

"Good," I echo. "Al, will you try to describe the sequence of this manual work."

"Chris, I'll need some help."

"Certainly, Al. I doubt if I know enough, but let's give it a try."

"Okay," Al starts. "The first step is very clear. The scheduler and the assembly superintendents decide on the schedule of our 'Herbie,' the paint shop."

"Yes," adds Chris. "We have created a nice, big wooden chart on the wall for this purpose."

"Jonah, how can we mechanize this first step," says Al. "I've been racking my brain for quite some time, but it's clearly beyond me."

"Can't our current MRP software do it?" asks Bert.

"No. And it's not just our MRP," answers Al, "but any MRP. You see Bert, one of the basic assumptions of MRP is infinite capacity, which in other words means internal constraints do not exist. If they do exist, as in our case and probably many other cases, then you are on your own!"

"That's not entirely accurate," Chris remarks. "You are supposed to handle these internal capacity constraints through changing the dates and quantities required at the upper levels—the final products. This is actually what is meant by the 'Master Schedule'. As a matter of fact that is exactly what we do in the second step of our manual procedures. Based on the schedule that we construct for the paint shop, we update our truck shipping schedule. This is simply a detailed procedure to create a Master Schedule, nothing more."

"Yes, I guess you're right," replies Al. "But I still don't know how to mechanize it."

"And try not to fall into the trap of considering the process time in calculating the overall lead time."

"Why should you?" asks Chris. "This is not a time consuming step. Moreover, the superintendents like to do it themselves. It gives them the feeling that they are in charge." After a short while he continues. "As a matter of fact, I want this critical step to be under their control, I myself will feel much better. No, Al, this is not the problem. The vast majority of the manual work and all the stupid mistakes, are in the next step where we determine the timing of the release of the thousands of components."

Al thinks for a minute or two. Everybody is silent, letting him self-digest this.

Finally he says, "I guess that this can be done by our current system, even though I will have to hammer out the details." And then, turning to me, he asks, "I understand that I will have to incorporate the buffer time into the MRP lead time. But this will increase the overall lead time." And, without waiting for an answer, he concludes, "I guess I will have to study the mechanism of Drum-Buffer-Rope again. It's already apparent that I'll have to erase most of the lead times that now are specified for the various levels."

"You are right," I say. "And try not to fall into the trap of considering the process time in calculating the overall lead time."

"Why?" asks Al. "I thought this would give us more precise answers than we get today."

"Don't forget that MRP assumes that the transfer batch is equal to the process batch."

"Don't forget that MRP assumes that the transfer batch is equal to the process batch. It might considerably distort the release," I add.

"What do you mean by those terms?" asks Chris.

"It's okay," says Al. "I'll explain it to you later. But, Jonah, how can we neglect the actual process time?"

"The buffers must be much larger than the process time of a single unit. I assume that today you are using weeks for the time buffers. What is the actual process time, on the average, for a single unit going through the shop?"

"No more than two hours at the most," answers Chris.

"I see," says Al. "But it is still very hard to swallow. To ignore all process times! Hmmm—I'll have to think about it."

Bert wasn't listening at all to the last part of the conversation. He is deep in thought. Chris looks a little bit puzzled, while J.P. is definitely bored.

But then Bert starts again, "If we cut the time allotted to manufacturing then we will not be able to tolerate any slippage in the release of drawings. Today, we don't have this problem since manufacturing is using most of their shorter lead times to give more leeway to preparation. They release the material much later than scheduled. J.P., I knew that your area must improve."

J.P. is no longer bored and a tense expression now forms on his face when Bert continues. "We must look in more detail into your area."

"What do you mean exactly?" asks J.P., still surprised by the sharp shift in the conversation.

"Do your people release the complete details of the order to manufacturing all at once, or are there almost always some drawings that are released much later?"

"You know the situation," answers J.P. "There are always, for some reason or another, some problem details that take longer to complete."

"Yes," says Bert. "And there is more than enough time allotted to complete them as well."

"Not with the existing CAD system."

"Here we go again," Bert says in a quite low tone. And then looking at the statistics that he holds in his hand he continues, "What is this two weeks to get the approval from the client? If he is pressed for time we certainly can ask him to approve it in two days. Especially when most of the approval is done piecemeal anyhow, during the four weeks that it takes us to do the drawings."

"Yes, that is right," says J.P., "but this is your instruction."

"Mine?!" explodes Bert.

"but this is your instruction."

"Mine?!" explodes Bert.

"Yes. You remember. Three years ago, when we had the debate with Olson and we had to replace a lot of furniture because some signatures were missing. You instructed us to allow two weeks for this stage and to make sure that every drawing is signed by the client."

"Yes, I do remember. But it was different then. Our problem at that time was capacity, not orders."

Bert looks angry and confused.

"Bert," J.P. speaks in a pacifying tone, "we were stressing the need for quoting reliable lead times. I don't see any problem of putting only two days for approval in our bids and adding a small section that clearly states that any delay in client approval, will delay the completion of the installation by the same number of days."

"Thank you," says Bert, "I appreciate it." But then after a short while he continues, "Can't we squeeze more time from the preparation?"

"Not with our current technology," answers J.P. in a rigid tone, careful not to show his impatience. "All my people are working all the time. I simply cannot see how we can squeeze anything more out, without giving them better tools."

Bert looks at me seeking help. "J.P.," I start. "Would you say that on the desk of your engineers we will find only the work that they are currently engaged in, or an additional job or two?"

"Since so many times a job is stuck due to some details that have to be clarified with someone else, we are very careful to supply everyone with more than one job. This is the only way that we can make everyone efficient. I would guess that on the desk of each of my people you will find at least two or three jobs."

J.P. looks quite satisfied with his answer, and he is surprised that Bert isn't.

"J.P., have you tried to look at the situation from the point of view of the jobs?" asks Bert.

"What do you mean," is J.P.'s puzzled response.

"If on each table there are two or three jobs," Bert tries to clarify, "then each job is waiting to be processed more time than it is actually processed."

"Try it on me once again. I don't see your point."

Bert looks at him in the attempt to find a better way to explain but at last he asks, "Have you read *The Goal*?"

"Yes, about two years ago," replies J.P. "But it's about manufacturing. What does it have to do with our preparation efforts which mainly engineering and paper work?"

Bert shows that a president must know the art of patience.

> *"Have you viewed The Goal in a more generic way? As a story about completing a task using a number of different resources?"*

"Have you viewed *The Goal* in a more generic way? As a story about completing a task using a number of different resources?"

"To tell the truth, no," answers J.P. "I'll have to read it again."

"Why don't you do it and then we will discuss the situation further," Bert concludes.

He starts to rise from his chair. "It was certainly a very fruitful day."

• • •

As Bert accompanies me to the lobby, he continues to speak about the events of the day. Finally, when we are at the front door he asks, "Jonah, are you satisfied with what we accomplished?"

"Yes, definitely," I answer. "Provided that you are aware that the most important question is still open."

"What do you mean?"

"Why did you need me to trigger the discussion? Why didn't you do it on your own?"

"Come on Jonah," Bert bursts into laughter. "I don't fool myself. If it wasn't for your pointed questions we would still be debating this thing and going in circles as we have done for the last six months."

"Yes, I see. But why couldn't you do the same on your own?"

Bert puts his big hand on my shoulder, "Not everyone is as gifted as you are, Jonah."

it is not a gift, it's just a skill honed by practicing some very specific techniques,

I turn to face him. "Bert, it is not a gift, it's just a skill honed by practicing some very specific techniques, like cause-and-effect reasoning to find the root cause problems and the 'evaporating clouds' technique to come up with those 'common sense' solutions." (See Issue 2 of the *Theory of Constraints Journal*). "My recommendation is that you invest some time learning and mastering them."

"Is it possible?" Bert asks in a totally unconvinced tone.

"Yes, it definitely is!" I answer.

Before we try to answer the crucial question postulated at the end of the article, "but why couldn't you do the same on your own?" maybe this is the appropriate place to summarize what the Theory of Constraints is.

USING THE TERMINOLOGY OF THE SYSTEM TO BE IMPROVED

THE FOCUSING PROCESS IS TO:

1. Identify the system's constraints.
2. Decide how to exploit the system's constraints.
3. Subordinate everything else to the above decision.
4. Elevate the system's constraints.

5. If in the previous step a constraint is broken, go back to step 1, but do not allow inertia to cause a system constraint.

USING THE TERMINOLOGY OF THE IMPROVEMENT PROCESS ITSELF

THE FOCUSING PROCESS IS:

1. What to change?
   —Pinpoint the core problems!
   —Effect-Cause-Effect method.
2. To what to change to?
   —Construct simple, practical solutions!
   —Evaporating Clouds method.
3. How to cause the change?
   —Induce the appropriate people to invent such solutions!
   —Socratic method.

PART TWO

HOW SHOULD IT BE IMPLEMENTED?

all our inventions/ decisions/convictions are based only on intuition (the communication of this to ourselves and others is based on logic).

As long as we understand that the Theory of Constraints is a process of ongoing improvement, then the situation described in *The Goal*, certainly should not be taken as an example. In *The Goal*, Alex has the responsibility and Jonah, the catalyst, is an external person. If we strive to just improve, to just turn a company from the red to the black, then this combination might work. But unfortunately this combination guarantees stagnation in the long-run and thus should not even be considered when the objective is to move an entire organization into a process of *ongoing* improvement. Why is this so? What we have to fully appreciate is the fact that all our inventions/decisions/convictions are based only on intuition (the communication of this to ourselves and others is based on logic). Intuition doesn't just grow out of thin air. Intuition stems from past experience. How much intuition do we have in nuclear physics, if we've never had any experience in that field?

In *The Goal*, at the outset, both Alex and Jonah have the intuition which is needed to improve Alex's plant. Alex from the experiences gained in his particular plant, Jonah from his experience gained in observing so many plants. You see, conventional plants are very similar to each other even though they differ dramatically in their details. Just ask yourself whether or not *The Goal* was written about your specific plant? Most readers claim that they can almost name the characters. As long as our organizations use the same distorted measurements and as long as management is trained to think in approximately the same way, it is no wonder that organizations are approximately the same.

So at the start, Jonah does possess the necessary intuition. He guides Alex, using the Socratic method, to find his own core problems and then guides him to find simple, practical solutions. Alex, armed with the powerful emotion of the inventor, succeeds in implementing his ideas in a surprisingly short period of time. He breaks the current constraint and the wheel of the improvement process makes a full turn. Now Alex's plant is not so conventional anymore; it is now much more unique. Jonah being external, not a part of the organization, does not benefit from the resulting elevation in intuition and thus his task, as a catalyst, becomes much more difficult. He cannot guide Alex over the phone anymore or through remote short meetings, now he must come to the plant. Once again the process repeats itself. Through questions, Alex is guided to turn the wheel once again. Now the plant is even more unique and Jonah's task—being external—becomes more and more an impossibility.

A good Jonah will be able to help an Alex Rogo turn the improvement wheel, maybe three times. An exceptional Jonah might succeed in doing it four times. I don't believe that there is anybody external to a plant, who can turn the wheel more than five times. What happens when the plant becomes so unique that Jonah, leaning on his intuition which is derived from the general cases, misreads the situation? In such circumstances, misreading will not be just a small glitch, Jonah will misread it by a mile. Let's remember, Jonah is guiding Alex through questions not through answers. What is the chance that Alex will figure out his perceived core problem? A problem which does not exist in reality, but only in the mind of Jonah. Alex having the correct, healthy intuition simply will not be able to ever find this erroneous core problem. Now the Socratic approach turns on the one who used it.

Just imagine Alex in this situation. He is so eager to find the answers; it is so important to his plant, and he fails. How many weeks do you think will pass, before Alex will become so frustrated, that he will grab Jonah by the throat and say something like, "okay, so I'm totally dumb, now give me the answers." Jonah, afraid for his life, will abandon the Socratic method and spell out his erroneous conclusion. We should not expect a very polite response from Alex, who guided by his healthy intuition will immediately spot the mistake. The result, a wall of mistrust, is built between Alex and Jonah. But can Alex find his core problems on his own? Can he construct simple, practical solutions on his own? Remember, Jonah has only guided him to find specific solutions, he didn't expose Alex to the focusing techniques at all.

Unable to pinpoint the next constraint, Alex will revert to continuing to improve the things that he knows how to improve—the previous constraints, which have already been broken. The plant's performance will now go into stagnation, which is the exact opposite of what we originally set out to achieve—a process of ongoing improvement.

The conclusion is quite clear. Alex and Jonah must not be two different people. Alex must be Jonah at the same time that he is Alex. It is not a matter of learning oceans of data, examining many cases or studying by heart numerous procedures. Fortunately, almost each of the managers in an organization has already acquired enough intuition. Intuitively we do know the problems, we even feel the simple solutions.

What is missing is the ability to verbalize our intuition, to provoke it, focus it and cast it precisely into words. The five steps of the Theory of Constraints, the Effect-Cause-Effect and the Evaporating Clouds methods are relatively easy to adopt, since they are totally in line with our intuition. It is just a matter of some practice which is especially geared towards unleashing their usage in a very broad spectrum of subjects, otherwise we'll continue to narrow the scope of TOC to production only.

What is missing is the ability to verbalize our intuition, to provoke it, focus it and cast it precisely into words.

Unfortunately, this is not the case with regards to the Socratic method itself. This method is counter-intuitive, not that we do not all recognize its validity, but when we are struggling to pinpoint a problem and then succeeding to even outline a solution, the temptation to show off and to spell out in detail our solution, is immense. We need considerable self-discipline to give, in such situations, just the questions and to refrain from giving the answers, while our audience is floundering. And then to watch how others take full ownership of our brain child. If this is not counter-intuitive then it is certainly counter to common behavior.

Using the Socratic approach is even more important, than previously perceived, when we take into account the fact that in Western organizations—in spite of all the lip service—entrepreneurial spirit at the medium and lower ranks is not, exactly, encouraged. Due to this "culture," the medium and lower ranks take upon themselves many limitations that the top management never intended to impose. Let's remember that as far as action is concerned, what you think is not so important; what your people think you think, that's what really counts.

what you think is not so important; what your people think you think, that's what really counts.

Bearing in mind management's inexperience in using the Socratic approach along with the absolute need of the troops to use their intuition, we have constructed a very large set of Socratic tools. These tools are in the form of computer simulations—almost games—which are thoroughly backed by detailed tutor guides. These simulations have been designed to help us verbalize our intuition when it is in contradiction with our erroneous, formal policies. Thus these tools cover a whole myriad of topics—rework situations, market segmentation, distribution, logistics, line layout, etc.

1. *How to Become a Jonah*

The formal rules and the Socratic tools enable a person to become a Jonah within a period of ten days. This is the Jonah Course. The first day is devoted primarily to shattering the accepted perceptions of our organization's reality, by expressing and analyzing the contradictions in the measurement system. Then we embark on a process of building self-confidence—building the ability to rely on one's own brain power and experience. The first thing to learn is the importance of proper terminology. For that we use an example of a process line. The saying "the line is down" is quite well defined, but what about the uptime of a line? Pointed questions, backed with a simulation, expose the lack of focus and relative uselessness of today's approach. Just by introducing the proper terminology, the students are able to derive on their own, workable procedures that enhance the Throughput of a line significantly. They also devise small practical changes that enhance significantly the other capabilities of a line.

To ruin the students' respect for the written word.

The subject of proper line design, which is vastly different from the existing concept of line balance, is wide open. The homework for the first night is designed to ruin the students' respect for the written word. The students have to come up with the analysis of Alex Rogo's mistakes and their devastating ramifications, as can be deduced from *The Goal.*

In the second day the line simulations are still used but this time the emphasis is on multi-purpose lines, in an effort to knock down the devastating artificial walls between functions. The students reveal to themselves how changing the logistical considerations, as regards to setup, can have far reaching ramifications on line design as well as distribution and marketing tactics. Once this is accomplished, a second round starts, this time on a more complicated environment. An "A" type organization is used, in a different type of simulation designed to teach the students the verbalization process by turning the generic three first steps (identify, exploit and subordinate) into practical working solutions. The Effect-Cause-Effect method is taught and practiced through homework.

The third day starts with an assault on some longstanding policy constraints. This is achieved by imposing those policy constraints on a simulated environment in which the student has struggled, on the previous day, to perfect. The devastating impact of these policy constraints serves to build the conviction in the students that they must rely on their own judgment, even in the face of longstanding, worldwide, accepted "truth."

Now the way is clear to start exposing the student to the meaning of elevating a constraint. Through a set of simulations the students reveal, analyze and learn to use the immense power of TQM and JIT techniques by focusing them properly rather than just using them (as done today) in a shotgun approach. The connections between production, local process improvements, engineering, marketing and most importantly finance is now emerging into a totally new, holistic pattern.

Now is the time to introduce the Evaporating Clouds method. This seemingly simplistic technique should not be underestimated and thus the homework is to use this technique to solve a major personal (non-industrial) problem. The next morning, the students are usually somewhat embarrassed. It turns out that we are far from even being able to express our problems precisely.

But team efforts elevate each student's abilities to new heights and some fascinating, sometimes ingenious, solutions usually emerge. At this crucial point, most of the students are starting to grasp the ramifications of what they are learning on their own. It is not just technical, it is not just aimed at improving their organizations, it has far-reaching ramifications on they themselves. As an anticlimax, the students develop the control mechanism needed to ensure that whatever improvements are made, they will not deteriorate as a result of the daily fire fighting. Now the inertia issue is confronted and rule number five of the Theory of Constraints is understood much more deeply than before. The homework for this night depends heavily on the composition of the specific class, but usually it involves analyzing a text through the combined power of the Effect-Cause-Effect, the Evaporating Clouds and the Socratic methods.

Making sure that each step will not cause any resistance in other groups, resistance that will jeopardize the implementation of the next steps.

On Friday after the students have had the chance to criticize the homework of the previous night, presented by some "volunteers," marketing problems are presented and analyzed, according to their impact when viewed through the other functions of the organization. Then the concept of implementation is introduced using the Effect-Cause-Effect method to determine the core problem and to present it in a way in which the proof is evident. Using the Evaporating Clouds method to find a simple solution. Then using the above analysis to identify the appropriate people who should be induced to implement specific sections of the overall solution.

The timing of the implementation steps is discussed with particular attention given to the ramifications of the organizations psychology. Making sure that each step will not cause any resistance in other groups, resistance that will jeopardize the implementation of the next steps. The homework for the weekend, for each student is, of course, to outline in detail the implementation plan for his/her actual area of responsibility.

The second week is heavily dependent on the particular functions and levels of the course participants. Each morning is devoted to an examination of several of their implementation plans. The critique is done mainly by the students themselves, where the tutor interferes only to ensure that the focus is maintained at all times. As it turns out, we are much more capable of finding mistakes in someone else's work than in our own. As a result of the students' own critiques, everyone realizes the mistakes and slippages that they themselves have done in their own work. It's no wonder that every evening, throughout the week, the students are busy rewriting their own implementation plans over and over again.

The afternoons are devoted to further exercise and expand the verbalization ability that the students have found in themselves. This is done primarily through exploring additional applications of the Theory of Constraints. To strengthen the emerging understanding, that our organizations are constrained currently not by physical constraints but mainly policy constraints, the whole subject of distribution is analyzed in-depth. The environment in which products are sold, not directly to the end customer, but through a network of warehouses and through intermediate distribution chains (which have their own network of warehouses). This environment currently exhibits an impressive list of devastating policy constraints.

Another case, which is analyzed in-depth, is a real life case of handling a network of independent distributors. This case was chosen because it does not contain even a trace of the original environment through which most people have been introduced to the Theory of Constraints—the shop floor described in *The Goal.* The extensive usage of the Effect-Cause-Effect, Evaporating Clouds and the Socratic methods prevents the students from connecting the usage of these methods to any particular environment.

The other topics covered are heavily dependent on the particular interest of the students and may range from "V," "A" and

"T" configuration analysis, to market segmentation analysis, to applications of the Theory of Constraints in product design or paper flow or devising local performance measurements or even the way in which we can use standard MRP to schedule the shop floor.

without a written *implementation plan, organizations seem to drift into stagnation.*

The emphasis throughout the week is, of course, on the ability to construct a practical solid implementation plan. This is of utmost importance since not only does the implementation plan, by definition, encompass all the various aspects of using the Theory of Constraints, but we have also found that without a *written* implementation plan, organizations seem to drift into stagnation.

Usually an implementation plan is developed in light of the current constraints and the best estimation of the next wave of constraints. The implementation itself usually turns out to be faster than we previously perceived possible. Since it is impractical to try to develop one implementation plan that will cover the first, second and even the third wave of constraints, there is the need to roll the implementation plan forward, on a relatively frequent basis. That's why it is so important that the students will acquire the ability to do it on their own, which brings us to a very interesting question.

Does an outside consultant have any role at all in this process? As it turns out the answer is definitely yes, provided we will change drastically what we expect from an external consultant. We shouldn't use an external consultant because he/she has more knowledge than we do, or because he/she has better analytical skills or better presentation skills. We should use external consultants because they know less, and not more, than we do. How is it that we reached such an unusual conclusion? As we said before, intuition stems from the daily experiences of life and when an organization embarks on a process of ongoing improvement, it becomes very unique making it very difficult to find matching intuition elsewhere.

not because he knows more or has a broader base of experience, but because he is not attached to the rooted assumptions—the inertia of the organization.

Everyone who has become a Jonah is painfully aware of the devastating impact of inertia and the magnitude of its grip. This inertia tends to degrade considerably any implementation plan. The last week of the Jonah course reveals to each participant just how much his implementation plan can be helped, by questions coming from people who do not know and are not part of his environment. People, that because they are not part of it, do not have the resulting devastating inertia.

Can anybody from the outside be used? The answer is yes, as long as this person is totally in sync with the verbalization-communication methods of the internal Jonahs. In other words, let's not forget that the Effect Cause Effect method has changed dramatically the meaning of the word *proof.* The Evaporating Clouds method has changed the meaning of the word *solution.* The Socratic method has changed the meaning of the verb *to induce* and the TOC as a whole has changed drastically the meaning of the verb *to focus.* Thus, an external consultant helping an internal Jonah, must be himself a Jonah and he should be called in whenever the internal implementation plan is being rolled. Called in, not because he knows more or has a broader base of experience, but because he is not attached to the rooted assumptions—the inertia of the organization. He should not be called in to help in devising or even in executing the implementation plan, but in order to scrutinize and shoot holes in it. When inertia is involved, we run the risk that reality won't do it and as a result significant opportunities will be passed by without anybody ever realizing it.

2. *The Devastating Impact of the Organization's Psychology*

The next myriad of questions is almost self-evident. Who should be the Jonahs in the organization? How many of them? Who first? And so on. Maybe the best way to answer these types of questions is to start right at the beginning. What do we really want to achieve? The implementation of a process of ongoing improvement in our organization!

For everyone who has read *The Goal,* it is obvious that there are only three avenues open through which we can improve the performance of an organization. To increase Throughput (sales), to decrease Inventory (assets) or to decrease Operating Expense. As far as an ongoing process is concerned, we mustn't look just for the immediate improvements, but we must also concentrate on the long-run. For the long-run it's obvious that the avenues of reducing Inventory and Operating Expense provide only a very limited number of opportunities—these two measurements are limited by zero. Throughput, on the other hand, we want to increase—no inherent limitations. Thus it's no wonder, that whenever a process of ongoing improvement is concerned, Throughput becomes the most important avenue.

What we know, all too well, is that the avenue of increased Throughput can be blocked by any function in our organization. In the long run every function—marketing, sales, distribution, production, materials, engineering or finance—every one of them, on its own, can block the Throughput channel.

Let's first examine the case, where at least one function is not on a process of ongoing improvement, either because this function doesn't really want to improve or because people don't know how to improve—it doesn't really matter why. What matters is, the fact, that in such a case it is only a matter of time until this function will block the Throughput avenue of the entire organization. Simply, the other functions, by improving will break the constraints that they can break. After a while, the only constraints which will govern the organization's Throughput will be the ones that need the active improvement of the function which is stagnant.

In such a situation, we can expect that the pressure of the organization to continue to improve will be channeled into the other two avenues which are still open—reduction of Inventory and Operating Expense. But let's not fool ourselves, only one avenue is actually open. The magnitude by which we can reduce our total Inventory is very limited. Material inventory is usually not an overwhelming portion of our total Inventory (assets), and the other assets cannot be easily reduced—what are we going to do, dump our machines? As for the material inventory—it is usually reduced significantly in a relatively short period of time and any further reduction will have only a limited impact on the total assets. The need to further reduce work-in-process and finished-goods inventories does not stem from the direct impact of reducing assets, but from the indirect—very important—impact it has on our potential to increase sales—Throughput. But let's not forget that we are now dealing with a case, where the opportunity to increase sales is blocked by one function.

So it's no wonder that, in such a case, all the pressure to improve the organization's performance will eventually become focused on the only open avenue—reduction of Operating Expense. Let's face it—what is the real meaning of reducing Operating Expense? In real life terminology, it is just another name for laying off people. The other opportunities to reduce expenses are generally quite small and usually involve the cancelling of exactly those small expenses, that we spend in order to improve the abilities of our manpower. Thus, the pressure to reduce Operating Expense will inevitably be translated, in the end, into layoffs.

And thus, in the end, we will be forced to punish the ones who improved.

Who are the people most likely to be impacted by those layoffs? Most probably not the ones in the function that is now the constraint of the company. They are already overwhelmed with work and everybody is well aware of it. No, the pressure will be directed to the functions that seem to have excess manpower. Those are exactly the functions that made the most dramatic improvements. Now we will have to face a very unpleasant and distorted situation. Those functions, that have improved the most, are unable to utilize their people to support additional Throughput—the increase in Throughput is blocked by the other function that still sticks to its old, inefficient methods. And thus, in the end, we will be forced to punish the ones who improved.

From the above diabolic analysis, it is apparent that the heads of all functions must be totally on board. But maybe, we could start the process under one function, prove to ourselves its validity and then armed with the convictions stemming from the good results, we will be able to bring everybody else on board much more easily. This is probably the line of reasoning that has guided hundreds of plant managers, all over the world. Plant managers who were in charge of only the production and material functions and reported to a division which was also responsible for all the other functions. Reality has shown us that those expectations—bringing everybody on board due to the impressive results achieved in the plant—are unfortunately very naïve. An enormous number of such cases have encountered that dominant power, known as the psychology of the organization. Originally we thought that each organization is comprised of individuals and it is enough just to deal, properly, with the psychology of the individual. Unfortunately, the organization itself has its own psychology which is not equivalent to the psychology of its individuals.

In retrospect we all knew it a long time ago. Just talk to five people in an organization and then take these same people to a bar, you are talking to different people. How many times have you witnessed a committee reaching a decision that none of its members would have taken individually? The organization has its own psychology, which if we are not careful enough to take it into account will, in the long run, lead us into grotesque situations.

Too often, lately, we are approached by plant managers desperately seeking a way out of the division's final decision to lay off people. The request is not coming from financially troubled plants, on the contrary, most of them are now very profitable. In questioning these people, there is a common pattern which appears. In spite of all their efforts another function is still blocking the Throughput channel.

in most western organizations being above budget is also considered a crime.

Just to give you the most common story. Once the plant improved, the plant manager approached the divisional vice president of marketing, begging for more sales. This was originally done because the plant manager was looking for work for his people. How many times can you re-paint the plant? To our astonishment, the conventional answer, in such a case, is "what do you want from me, we are already thirteen percent over budget?" It turns out, that in most Western organizations being above budget is also considered a crime. In some cases—especially when the plant's performance was not improved based on *The Goal* alone, but the plant manager was also a Jonah—very extensive work was done in order to try and open the marketing channel. Sometimes, to the extent that a thorough market survey was done, segmented markets were defined and the bottom line analysis was shown. In almost all cases this was just done in vain, even with the carrot of much higher total commissions for the sales force.

This phenomena has been witnessed on such a grand scale, that we could no longer attribute it to the specific characteristics of the people involved. So we started to look for a deeper, more generic reason. Suppose that you are the head of production, for example, and another person is the head of marketing. In a hierarchical organization you are both competing for the same, next slot—your current boss's position. Now try to imagine that you have improved your area dramatically and for some time now you have been putting the pressure on the head of marketing to achieve more sales. Under such a scenario he feels criticized. Thus, what we can expect as a reaction is the defense mechanism—in the form of the many reasons why sales cannot be increased. Let's suppose that he will succeed in improving sales by some percentage points, what will the impact be on your measurements?

Remember, you have already improved, to the extent, that no constraints reside in production. Every single resource is definitely a non-constraint, thus you can satisfy the increase in sales without any increase at all in Operating Expense. The entire difference between your selling price and the price of raw materials will glide nicely and directly to the bottom line. This is certainly very good for the company as a whole. But let's not be blind to the fact that a slight improvement in marketing's performance gives by far a larger improvement to your results.

Put yourself in his shoes, would you try to overcome the seemingly, sound excuses of why sales cannot be increased?

Intuitively your peer recognizes that he is now facing a situation, where any improvement on his side, will increase your chances of promotion, more than his. Put yourself in his shoes, would you try to overcome the seemingly, sound excuses of why sales cannot be increased? To tell you the truth, we would prefer that this hypothesis is wrong. In fact, we prefer to think that people do put their company's interest above their own, so we were looking for another effect that must stem from this hypothesis, not in order to validate it, but to invalidate it.

Due to the plot chosen for *The Goal,* some applications of the Theory of Constraints to the production and material functions are obvious to everyone. *The Goal* hardly touches the applications for marketing, distribution, administration or design engineering. We assume that the openness of these functions to recognize and adopt the Theory of Constraints applications to their issues, will be enhanced by the positive results achieved in the other functions or at least unrelated to it, where the people involved will judge the subject matter on its own merit.

What we found out was that this is certainly not the case. When a company has not yet implemented the ideas of *The Goal* and all functions are exposed to the Theory of Constraints at approximately the same time, almost everyone is enthused by the applications and potential for their own function. Certainly there is no way to distinguish the response by function. But we do know that this is not the case, when *The Goal* implementation is already in place. In these cases, all our efforts to convince marketing and engineering didn't even make a dent. The emotional resistance, which already exists, prevents almost any meaningful dialogue. The only way to open the Throughput channel in these cases was through personnel changes.

The lesson today is loud and clear. Before any function can go on an ego trip, demonstrating and waving results (and by that digging its own grave)—before any function can start individual improvements, all functions should decide together on a common way.

3. *Reaching the Initial Consensus and the Initial Step*

All functions should buy in before any significant efforts to improve are allowed to start.

Pilots, even though successful locally, are not helpful at all in moving an entire organization. All functions should buy in before any significant efforts to improve are allowed to start. This is easy to say and it's not so hard to achieve. A very deep and broad consensus can be achieved through a two-day workshop, in which the heads of all the functions will participate. We call it the Executive Decision Making Workshop, in short, EDM.

The EDM develops the Theory of Constraints through the use of examples, which are of equal interest to all functions. It starts by demonstrating the importance of knowing "What To Change," proving that what stands between the participants and a total consensus on the core problems is just the ability to verbalize. The example used is the problems inherent in a hierchical pyramid structure and through the use of the Effect-Cause-Effect method, the lack of proper operational measurements is revealed. Then the importance of finding "To What To Change To" is examined and once again the power of verbalization is demonstrated, by exposing everyone to the fact their own intuition leads them to exactly the same conclusions, no matter in which function they had gained their experience. The five steps of the Theory of Constraints is eventually accepted to be valid, almost to the extent of "motherhood and apple pie."

Now it's time to demonstrate that as long as proper verbalization is not used, we ourselves will act in ways that contradict our own intuition. To achieve this, a numerical example is presented, where the participants will struggle to solve it on their own. This same example is also used to show the distance that exists between the participant's intuition and the formal system, with respect to any aspect of the business—product mix decisions, financial measurements, behavior on the shop-floor, sales commissions, process engineering activities, quality efforts, as well as investment and marketing strategies. All of the latter is exposed to the participants within one short hour. The interrelationships of the various functions is now clearly evident. The policies and culture of the organization are actually cross disciplinary.

The process of change is then discussed and the Socratic tools are presented. The audience is now experiencing the effectiveness of the Socratic tools on themselves. They are finding out just how much they enjoy being educated while at the same time how much they hate to be trained. Using the Socratic tools, the participants encounter the problems directly and develop the simple, practical solutions. They convince themselves of the short distance that exists between the generic rules of the Theory of Constraints and the development of the powerful, practical day to day procedures. In the process they gain a much deeper insight into the scope and depth of the Theory of Constraints. But even more importantly, the avenue through which to stimulate and educate the troops, in each function, is now clearly understood. After a thorough discussion of how to handle the psychology of an organization, the details of moving ahead, for the particular organization, are hammered out. And a true group consensus, amongst all functions, to embark on this common sense, but still daring process of ongoing improvement, is achieved.

If your company is a consumer products company, then what we recommend is to extend this workshop to include a third day. The reason is that these companies are currently suffering from a much larger myriad of policy constraints, as well as the fact that they make use of a larger and more industry specific terminology. Words like *promotion, shelf life* and *returns* are commonplace for such companies, where you will almost find them not used in any other type of industry.

Communication between marketing and production is virtually nonexistent and the finger-pointing syndrome is usually more intense here than in any other industrial environment.

The feedback loops in terms of the ramifications one function has on another, usually takes place through the clients (which in this environment are not the same people as the end consumers) and are of a nature where the time frame is very long. Ricochets usually hit another function only several months after the fact. Communication between marketing and production is virtually nonexistent and the finger-pointing syndrome is usually more intense here than in any other industrial environment.

To reach a group consensus in these environments usually takes a little more time (three days rather than two). We call this three day workshop CPM which stands for Consumer Products Management.

Now that we understand the necessity of having all the functions involved in the decision to embark on the Theory of Constraints, the avenue to begin answering the question of "who should be the Jonahs" is wide open. The minimum unit that can move ahead, without putting in the seeds of long term distortion, is what we call a division—a unit that contains all functions: marketing, sales, distribution, production, materials, design engineering and of course, finance. It should be noted that this definition doesn't imply anything about the size of a unit. It can be a privately held company of 20 people or an entire conglomerate where marketing and production meet only at the president's office.

It is very clear that the heads of all the functions must be Jonahs, but should they be the first Jonahs? Here again, we must refer back to the psychology of our organizations. It turns out, that there are some issues on which we are allowed or even expected to be right, but there are other issues which we are not even allowed to consider, let alone be right.

Suppose that you are the head of a function reporting to a boss who is in charge of multiple functions. In issues regarding only your function, you are expected to be right, but what about questions involving several functions? It is presumed that you should hold a narrow, local view while it is your boss who is the one who should see the entire picture. Therefore, with these types of questions, it is simply not healthy to be right, when your boss is wrong.

A Jonah is educated to examine any problem from the point of view of its global impact. What we have seen, from many cases where the head of a function is a Jonah and his boss is not (yes, his/her boss is very supportive or at least he/she was at the outset), is the Jonah, after a while, is either fired or becomes very frustrated from having to obey, what in his/her eyes, are totally irrational decisions.

The conclusion is obvious: the head of the division should be the first Jonah. He/she is the one who should constantly lead his/her company on a process of ongoing improvement. In going first, should they go by themselves? If a division and not a total company is concerned, then our recommendation is no.

There is one function that can, at almost any given point in time, block any other function . . . Finance.

There is one function that can, at almost any given point in time, block any other function. This is, of course, finance. The comptroller has another unique feature which the heads of the other functions do not have. He/she is the only one who has a very strong dotted line outside of the division. Sometimes this dotted line is stronger than the solid line to the head of the division. Besides, in almost all cases, the head of a unit and his/her comptroller are used to working as a very strong team. Add to it the fact that this function has to change its formal procedures the most, and will therefore need more lead time than the others, and the answer is obvious. The head of the division and his/her comptroller should be the first Jonahs of the unit.

Who second, third and so on? Here we can only give very general suggestions. It is quite evident the implementation itself should start with the function that can elevate the current constraints the most. This, however, is not always the function that controls the current constraints. For example, in a plant which is a "T" configuration, the market is the constraint, but this is the result of very poor due date performance. The constraint is under marketing, but the ones who can elevate it the most, are materials and assembly. Hence, the sequence in which the functions should start depends strongly on where the current constraints reside, who can elevate them, who can exploit and subordinate and where is the next wave of constraints going to reside.

Thus the detail answer to the question of who should be the second and third Jonahs, and so on, can be only given on a case by case basis. Who should decide? The idea is that the division head and the comptroller, in their Jonah course, should decide this as an integral part of their implementation plan. Thus, the recommended sequence for establishing a process of ongoing improvement is as follows. First, achieve a group consensus at the top of a division which includes all function heads. This group should then "send" the division head and the comptroller to the Jonah course as their "representatives." The division head and the comptroller will then prepare the implementation plan which also includes the sequence and timing of when each of the function heads are going to acquire the Jonah education. This implementation plan should then be brought back to the group for its "approval" before execution begins.

How deep in the organization should the Jonah education be given? This is not a trivial question, bearing in mind that all the Jonahs will have in their possession the Socratic simulations and the know how of how to use them, in order to unleash the intuition of the people reporting to them in a variety of situations. Remember, the goal of your organization is probably to make money, not to educate its people—this might be a means but certainly not the goal.

How deep in the organization should the Jonah education be given?

The answer to this question has only recently surfaced due to a phenomena that has become apparent during the last year. It turns out that the Socratic approach has a limited span of applicability. You yourself have probably noted that while reading *The Goal* and being on the receiving end of the Socratic approach you felt, alongside with the enthusiasm of the inventor, something not so sweet. You felt manipulated, almost lead by the nose. It turns out that using the Socratic approach continuously can enhance this bad feeling to the point of a crisis.

People who are positioned to have total responsibility for a section of the organization are the ones who feel it the most. It turns out, that, after they have been lead a few times by their Jonah to the realization (invention) of what they should do, there will come a time when their response to being led any farther is, "stop maneuvering me." "You put me in charge, let me manage." And these same people, who were initially so open and enthusiastic, were implementing the improvements and proud of the results they achieved, will after some time begin putting blocks in the way of any new improvement ideas. Their ownership of the responsibility takes precedence.

Their ownership of the responsibility takes precedence.

The only way we have found to overcome this phenomena is to give them the ability to invent on their own. The ability to use the focusing processes directly, without the constant detail guidance from above. Let's remember the Socratic method is essential only when a Jonah is trying to induce a non-

Jonah to invent. This is not the case, at all, between two Jonahs. The communication between them is already so precise (the meaning of proof, solution and focusing) that the Socratic approach is simply redundant or even disturbing. How deep should we take the Jonah education? The answer is now crystal clear. What is clear is that eventually we will need to bring it to the lowest level of our organization, where people feel totally responsible for their area—to the lowest level kings.

How can we identify a king? We all know. If you are the direct boss of a king and you will give direct instructions to his/her people, he/she will be extremely annoyed. You are supposed to go through them.

How can we make sure that we have identified the lowest level of kings? The hierarchical structure of our organization is not as arbitrary as many people might think. We have already constructed our organizations so that the lowest level king has the ability to put their hands around their people, to be fully aware of all the details occurring in their kingdom. This, by the way, produces different size kingdoms for different functions.

In production, for example, I don't believe that a person can put his arms around more than 200 people. If a person is managing more than 200 workers, it will be enough just to examine the management tree structure, to easily identify the kings below him/her.

But in design engineering, what we will find is that the lowest level king is in charge of not more than 15 design engineers. If a person is in charge of more than 15 design engineers, then he/she most probably knows what is happening only at the block diagram level and certainly he/she cannot be aware of all of the details of the design.

In sales the limit is probably not much larger than 6 or 7 salespeople. A person who is in charge of a larger number of salespeople is probably no longer aware of all the details of the proposals being given to the clients. At the same time we should remember, once again, that the goal of a company is to make more money and not to educate its employees.

Education is a means and not a goal, thus the investment in education should be viewed versus the amount of money a manager is responsible for.

Education is a means and not a goal, thus the investment in education should be viewed versus the amount of money a manager is responsible for. On this point we should be very careful not to fall, once again, into the trap of cost accounting. The amount of money that we mentioned above, is not the amount of Operating Expense spent in the area of a king, but the amount of Throughput dollars this manager impacts. Reviewing the Throughput dollars affected by each manager, will immediately show that 200 production workers, 15 design engineers and 7 salespeople certainly differ drastically where Operating Expense is concerned but they do each control about the same amount of Throughput dollars.

It should also be emphasized that there is no need to put all these managers—all these kings—through the Jonah course as fast as possible. As a matter of fact, it is not even recommended. When a manager goes through the Jonah course, he/she will outline as part of her implementation plan when the next, maximum two levels below her will need to take the same course. The timing depends strongly, not only on the speed in which the constraints are elevated, but even more so on the specific personalities of the people involved.

The initial investment is thus the investment to get the group consensus, and the education for the president and comptroller and the education given internally by them. Further investments should be financed by the already achieved improvements.

4. *How to Reach the Top*

Unless you are a divisional manager, you are probably saying to yourself at this stage, this is all well and good, but how can I persuade all of the top guys in my division to invest two days of their time in investigating the Theory of Constraints. My advice is that you first of all, clarify to yourself much more what does the Theory of Constraints mean to you and your organization.

This book, unlike *The Goal,* probably appeals more to your logic than to your emotions. You probably even agree with most of what is written here, but you don't "own" it. Do you have to, first of all, invest in the two days yourself? At this stage our experience shows that a less expensive and shorter investment of time is sufficient. The TOC seminars are a shorter (one day) version of the EDM. This might not be sufficient in reaching a total group consensus (where everyone counts), but for you who bothered to read this book to this point, it will be a stimulating and worthwhile experience.

But how can we help you to move the top guys? Bringing yourself to a TOC seminar, to become more convinced and more enthusiastic, does not seem as if it will have any impact on the top guys. Nevertheless, I thoroughly believe that people should not act based on artificial or partial knowledge. This step is, in my eyes, very important for you in hammering out your major concerns. Armed with a deeper understanding, please, don't make the mistake of now trying to persuade your boss.

Intuition, in this case, is misleading. The fastest way to get the attention of the top guy is not through the vertical line.

Try to imagine that you will go to your boss in the attempt of convincing him to go to his boss and so on.

Try to imagine that you will go to your boss in the attempt of convincing him to go to his boss and so on. Let's even suppose that your boss is favorably inclined, she was the one who gave you *The Goal* in the first place. Don't forget that her impression is that the Theory of Constraints is geared mainly to production. Her understanding is still at the level of bottleneccks and cutting batch sizes.

You're not a Jonah yet and your verbalization skills and your knowledge of how to use the Socratic approach is still far from sufficient. But suppose that you do succeed—miracles do sometimes happen—and now your boss has to face her boss. His level of understanding and thus his ability to explain will certainly not be sufficient. Most probably he will revert to using specific examples and references. The maximum that can be achieved in this way is a response of the sort, "it is very interesting and makes sense, I am fully supportive. Why don't you go ahead and implement it." This positive delegation has now blocked the essential need to start from the top. Remember, the above scenario is probably the best one, since the politics tend to become more and more fierce as you approach the top of the pyramid. In your frustration, don't even dream of writing a letter to the president. Such letters must go through the proper channels. If you will do it and your boss will find out about it, you can imagine her reaction. But if your boss's boss finds out about it, you will most likely have to visit your headhunter.

So what can you do about it? Are all avenues blocked? No, you are allowed to freely move sideways. So move sideways as much as you can. Contact somebody that belongs to another sub-unit and works in a function different than yours. If you are in production, contact somebody who works in engineering, marketing or finance, but not another person from production.

The more physically remote the other sub-unit, the better as well.

And then, don't even attempt to tell the other person that the way they are conducting their affairs is hurting your job. Don't even hint that what they are doing might be wrong. There is no point in starting by criticizing, it will only create a negative resistance. Approach it in the positive way. Tell him/her that you came across a method that makes a lot of sense to you, but the message was so heavily loaded with terminology that it is foreign to you. Terminology of their function, which you really don't fully understand, and therefore before you will consider to embrace this new method, you are asking for his opinion about it. You are basically asking him to invest some of his time, so that they can give you his best advice about the risks involved. Nobody can refuse such a request. Whenever, we are approached in a way that recognizes our knowledge and is highly regarding our opinion, somehow we all turn into purring pussycats.

> *now both of you together can do something, which is an impossibility for either of you to do on your own.*

If this other person is known to you as a daring, open-minded individual, ask him to go to the one day TOC seminar (of course after reading *The Goal* and giving you his initial thoughts). Otherwise try to minimize the risk by guiding him into one of the open EDM workshops. The chances are that he will come back not any less enthused than you are and now both of you together can do something, which is an impossibility for either of you to do on your own.

Without taking any risk, both of you together can write a letter directly to the divisional manager (remember the specific meaning of the word *division* used in this book). In this letter just highlight that you came across this theory that makes a lot of sense to each one of you but you both feel that it's vital that the divisional manager himself/herself will check it thoroughly. That's all. Both of you sign the same single letter, but before sending it, check with your direct bosses to see if it is all right. Their response in almost all cases will be the same. Just a faint smile about your naivety, but no objection. You see, there isn't any appropriate channel in the pyramid for a letter signed by two different functions belonging to two different sub-units. That's why nobody will block it and nobody will feel hurt that it wasn't channeled through them.

But when your letter will arrive to the division head it will have a real impact. You see, this person knows very well that two people from two different functions cannot agree on anything. That is his/her biggest problem and thus he/she will certainly not ignore it but start to investigate the subject matter. In our experience, which is based on many cases, there is a very high probability that both of you will be called by the division head for an hour or so meeting. By that time, you will have already internalized the message, to the extent that you probably won't have any problems coming out of this meeting high and tall. The ball is now exactly where it should be. The process will start without putting in the seeds of long term distortions.

If you do report directly to the division head, then, please, use the same technique. If you hold a staff position, first persuade one of your peers which is in a line position, and vice versa. Only then should both of you go to the division head.

5. *What About Existing New Projects?*

One of the still open questions is: what is the relationship between the Theory of Constraints and the other valid theories, or maybe techniques, that we have all recently become aware of—management philosophies like JIT and TQM? Can we adopt one without the other? Are they contradictory or complimentary and if so how? I think that my best and most honest opinion about this is expressed in the *Theory of Constraints Journal,* Volume 1, Number 6, Article 1, from which an extract appears in the following pages. As for the particular procedures needed to combine the specific and very technical techniques that each has developed, this part became totally apparent only after we clarified to ourselves, why these management theories are becoming more and more similar with each passing year.

When this happens, we will witness a movement that cannot be described in any other way, except as a renaissance.

Many times, in the history of science, a situation arises where the existing knowledge in a particular subject is no longer satisfactory. When this happens, we will witness a movement that cannot be described in any other way, except as a renaissance. In many places, independent and autonomic efforts will begin to break new ground. In the beginning, when these efforts are still in their infancy and resemble much more, new "beliefs" rather than substantiated, valid approaches—the community, extrapolating from the accepted body of knowledge, will relate to these new attempts as too avant-garde—strange, almost ridiculous and certainly doubtful ideas. It is no wonder that the originators, convinced of the validity of their intuition and still lacking a clear verbalization, will respond back with an attitude that will be rightfully referred to as arrogant or even fanatic.

This attitude of the originators—and the close groups that have already been convinced by them—tends to put them on a war path. Unfortunately, a fight which is not just against the established body of knowledge but one which is also against each other's ideas. Some—but certainly not sufficient—precautions will be taken by them, to recognize the good parts of the existing know-how; some half-hearted attempts not to throw the baby away with the bath water will be made. This, however, is usually not the relationship between the originators of the new and different ideas. Each has a very good understanding of the existing body of knowledge. Having analyzed it in depth, their new insights give them a very deep understanding into it. But, this is certainly not the case when they are relating to each other's ideas. The information at this stage is quite limited, the new ideas have not yet matured to the degree that they can be clearly explained. Thus it's no wonder that in retrospect it looks as if these people, in the name of open mindedness, are attacking each other's approaches with the zeal and biased logic of a fanatic.

Most of these new approaches usually provide a significant contribution. They may emerge from different angles, they may be based on different facets of the established base of knowledge. But this does not mean that only one of them is valid and all the others are wrong. It certainly doesn't imply that we have to choose one over the other or one at the exclusion of the others. It is no wonder that after some time the consolidation process must begin. People start to explore ways in which to mold the new ideas, which have passed the test of reality, into a new and uniform body of knowledge. We will find less and less articles, as well as presentations, entitled "this or that method—which is better?" But rather, synergetic attempts will start to be voiced.

This approach does not lead to synergism, but only to co-existence.

At this stage, an attitude of compromise begins to dominate the subject, where territorialism is the main guide of those "synergetic" efforts. We try to encompass them all, by dividing up their areas of application—this method is most suited for such a case, while this other method is more suitable when dealing with such symptoms. These compromises, even though calming the heated environment and providing the necessary conditions for meaningful communication, are at the same time, opening artificial gaps between the various, valid new methods. This approach does not lead to synergism, but only to co-existence, and as such postpones the most beneficial stage, that of molding all of the existing methods into one extremely powerful body of knowledge. A body of knowledge, in which internal conflicts have been resolved and the ground is ready for the next explosion of new ideas.

I believe that we should strive to highlight also the underlying differences, rather than just emphasizing the similarities, in order to achieve a meaningful synergy. Only in this way, where the different basic assumptions are exposed and analyzed, is there a realistic chance of achieving a single uniform theory. The different contributions, of each of these new methods, can then be amalgamated into one theory, which is even more powerful than just the summation of all the individual methods. The previous article (*Theory of Constraints Journal,* Volume 1, Number 5), which explains the existence of statistical fluctuations and dependent resources, as well as their impact, provides the framework in which such a powerful analysis can be carried out. An analysis of those new methods, that have tantalized management science for the last two decades.

It is quite obvious to everybody, that Just-In-Time (JIT), Total Quality Management (TQM) and the Theory of Constraints (TOC), all aim towards achieving the same objective, namely, to increase the ability of a company to make more money now, as well as in the future.

What is not so well understood, is that what differs between them is not the basic assumption that they attack—they all attack the same erroneous assumption. Moreover, they all use the same new assumption in place of the old one. The main difference between them lays more in the realization of the depth change which must stem from the assumption they use. Thus, of course, we will find the bigger differences in the techniques they have, or have not, developed to cope with the resulting change. It is very important to clearly verbalize these differences, otherwise the attempts to consolidate their derived, recommended actions, will be at best viewed as complimentary actions, rather than the constant enhancement of each other's methods within a single on-going, uniform implementation procedure.

Coming to clarify the existing maze, the first step should be the removal of the existing misconceptions, as to what is the primary problem that each one of these methods is struggling to solve. These misconceptions arise from the impressions that we all got, during the stage when these methods were in their infancy and only vaguely understood. Today, we have grown to learn that our initial impressions were much too limited and that each one of these . . . methods encompasses much more than what was originally envisioned. Still, it's very hard to overcome our inertia and to realize that a broader understanding of each one of these methods clearly indicates that they are all dealing directly, with exactly the same problem. In order to realize, not only the magnitude by which our perceptions of these methods has changed in the last few years, but that in all cases our perceptions have also evolved in basically the same direction, it might be worthwhile to put into one paragraph, what we all used to say sporadically.

"It's not enough to state that Just-In-Time's primary focus is not the reduction of inventory, it's not just a mechanical KANBAN System, but it's definitely an overall management philosophy." "It's not enough to state that Total-Quality-Management's primary focus is not the increase of the quality of our products, it's not just a procedural SPC system, but it's definitely an overall management philosophy." "It's not enough to state that the Theory of Constraints' primary focus is not the elevation of bottlenecks on the shop floor, it's not just a mechanical DBR system, but it's definitely an overall management philosophy."

being satisfied with broad statements like: "overall philosophy"— certainly doesn't provide a feasible starting point from which to consolidate these methods.

I don't think that anybody has a quarrel with the above paragraph, but what must be emphasized is that, in spite of the fact that we have come to realize the broader scope of these methods, no significant efforts have been made to re-state the problems that they do address. Saying, that what we originally understood, focus of these methods to be, was much to narrow, is important, but it does not by itself clarify what their primary focus is. Leaving the situation unchanged and being satisfied with broad statements like: "overall management philosophy"—certainly doesn't provide a feasible starting point from which to consolidate these methods.

The mere fact that no such restatement of their primary focus has been suggested clearly indicates that it's not a trivial task. I believe that the obstacle to such a restatement resides in the fact that even the original problem, which they all have tried to re-solve, cannot be found within the old body of knowledge. We can derive that problem only from the new angle provided by the new methods.

Being most familiar with TOC, I will naturally use its termi-nology, in my effort to highlight what, I think, is the common original problem. At the same time I'm sure that equivalent clarification can be made using JIT or TQM terminology.

In our efforts to restate, precisely, the problem these methods addressed, it's obvious that we have to, first of all, state their desired objective. A problem exists, only when we encounter something that prevents or limits our ability to achieve a desired objective. In our case we don't have to differentiate between the various methods at this stage, because as we already noted, they all have exactly the same objective. To improve the ability of a company to make more money now, as well as in the future.

Which avenue offers the biggest opportunity?

How can we improve the ability of a company to make more money? The Theory of Constraints clearly states what is obvious to everyone: there are only three avenues open to increase money making. The three avenues are: (1) to increase Throughput, (2) to decrease Inventory and (3) to decrease Operating Expense.

Which avenue offers the biggest opportunity? If we look just at the short term, the answer will be that Throughput and Operating Expense are equal in importance and both are more important than Inventory. This impression stems from the way Throughput (T), Inventory (I) and Operating Expense (OE) appear in the relationships most often used to judge "making money." Throughput and Operating Expense both appear in the Net-Profit and in the Return on Investment calculations, where Inventory appears only in the latter. And in both relationships, Throughput and Operating Expense are considered to have the same degree of importance, since they enter these relationships through difference between them.

$$NP = T - OE \qquad\qquad ROI = (T - OE)/I$$

Actually, our traditional scale of importance is slightly different. In the short run, it looks as if our ability to impact Operating Expense is much higher than our ability to increase Throughput. We don't control the market, but we do run our own show. This perception, by itself, is enough to place Operating Expense on a higher level than Throughput, but this tendency is intensified considerably by the other measurements that we use.

Most of the factors impacting our ability to increase Throughput are currently called intangibles.

The measurement that dominates our short and medium term behavior is cost accouting. What is "cost" if not Operating Expense? And thus, by the mere fact that cost considerations are used for any type of medium range decision, Operating Expense becomes more emphasized than Throughput. Let's remember, that most of the factors impacting our ability to increase Throughput are currently called—intangibles.

The impact of cost accounting on the importance of Inventory is even more dramatic. The way we evaluate material inventory enables us to disguise part of our Operating Expense as Inventory. This mechanism completely disguises the importance of Inventory. In using the avenue of reducing Inventory, we no longer know if we actually made "more money" or maybe we achieved just the opposite.

Thus until these new methods appeared on the scene, in a significant way, we witness, that in spite of top management's healthy intuition, that the reality of our companies has been such that Operating Expense held the driver's seat. Throughput in most cases was just a second contender, while Inventory trailed way behind, giving the impression that maybe it wasn't even in the race.

All three methods, TQM, JIT and TOC, since their conception, did not accept this ranking. They have all recognized that for the long run (making money also in the future) it's essential to adopt an entirely different ranking. This recognition was initially only an intuitive recognition, as can be easily deduced from examining the early publications. I certainly can attest to it personally, as far as the Theory Of Constraints is concerned. But the struggle to convince the market of the validity of this new approach leads to a better verbalization. Today, after years of struggle, the new scale of importance has become so widely accepted, that probably, in a few years, we will all have a hard time remembering that there once was a time when we actually did accept the old one.

When we come to evaluate which avenue (T, I or OE) presents more opportunities for improving the long run, the answer is obvious. In striving to decrease OE and I, the magnitude of improvement available is, by definition, limited since both of them cannot exist in the range of negative numbers. But this is not the case for T, this measurement, which we strive to increase is, inherently, unlimited. When it comes time to judging the performance of a specific period, T and OE are on the same level of importance, nevertheless, when it comes time to evaluating what we should do, in order to increase the ability of the company to make money on an on-going basis, T definitely takes a first and foremost position.

What about the relationship between OE and I? Which one of them is more important? At first sight it looks as if there is no valid reason to change our previous analysis. But this is definitely not the case. In our previous analysis, we have considered only the direct impact of these measurements on the financial relationships (NP and ROI).

What was neglected in this analysis was the parallel indirect impact that inventory has on the financial relationships. Even in the traditional body of knowledge it is recognized that such indirect channels exist. The carrying cost of material and the depreciation of assets have always been taken into account. In other words, it is very well recognized that Inventory does have an indirect impact on Net-Profit through its impact on OE.

A channel through which material inventory impacts not only OE, but more importantly, future Throughput.

What all the three new methods were fighting so zealously, to bring formally to the attention of management, is the importance of another indirect channel. A channel through which material inventory impacts not only OE, but more importantly, future Throughput. All the new methods have claimed that this long neglected channel is immensely important and should not be possibly discarded, whenever our future ability to sell in the market, is concerned.

I believe that the way in which all three methods regard the indirect channel, through which Inventory impacts Throughput, is well documented in *The Race* (pages 34–67). In those pages, it is proven that the work-in-process and the finished-goods portion of the Inventory, has a dramatic impact on the future Throughput of a company.

The future Throughput of a company is determined mainly by its ability to compete in the market. The parameters that dominate a company's competitive edge are: its products (both the quality and the engineering aspects), the price (which translates into margins and investment per unit) and responsiveness (due-date performance, as well as quoted lead times). All three methods point to the fact, that material inventory has a devastating impact on all of the above parameters, and thus to enable the increase of Throughput in the future, it is vital to reduce inventory in the present.

We see that the scale of importance that all the new methods are using is drastically different from the one that was assumed by the previous bodies of knowledge. Rather than considering OE as the number one avenue for improvement, T as number two and I as a doubtful third, the more correct scale is: T is definitely first, I is second (due to its indirect impact on future T) and OE is just a close third.

The uncompromising stand that all these methods have taken, to highlight the importance of this scale, is what caused a distortion in the perception of the main message these methods tried to advocate. For several years we were misled into believing that the main objective of the Total Quality Management was to improve customer service and product quality.

No wonder that TQM was so zealous about those issues, otherwise we would have continued to justify investment to improve Throughput, primarily on the incorrect basis of cost savings (OE). Only recently have we succeeded in breaking this all too narrow perception of TQM.

Otherwise we would have continued to justify investments to improve quality, primarily on the incorrect basis of cost savings (OE).

The same has happened to our perception regarding JIT. It wasn't too long ago that the crusade to move companies along the lines of this method was called: "Zero-Inventory." Even today JIT is still described as the method that regards Inventory as a liability. I wonder how anybody was led to believe the JIT is advocating reduction of inventory even on the expense of current customer service. Now it is obvious to everybody that the emphasis placed by JIT on inventory-reduction was only done for the purpose of improving future Throughput.

As for the TOC—it took a slightly different punishment. In its efforts to put OE in its proper place of importance, this method launched a crusade against the accepted principles of cost accounting. The undesirable result was that, until recently, this crusade was regarded, by many, as the main thrust of TOC.

Like every practitioner, they were keenly aware that the primary way to protect the current Throughput is through building material Inventory.

Now, that we have clarified, that all three methods agree on the same goal and on the same (different) scale of importance . . . for the measurements, the ground is set to verbalize the common problem which caused this misconception. The problem stems from their realization of the important role material inventory reduction plays, in the ability to increase future Throughput. All three methods, being extremely pragmatic, did not take the shortcut of just stating blindly "reduce inventory" (even though many of their followers have mistakenly espoused this idea). Like every practitioner, they were keenly aware that the primary way to protect the current Throughput is through building material Inventory. What are the KANBAN cards of JIT, and the Time-Buffers of TOC, if not a deliberate effort to build material inventory? Zero-inventory is synonymous only with zero-production and thus zero-Throughput. Not having inventory buffers is equivalent to the ridiculous declaration that Murphy does not exist.

This recognition, of the two conflicting influences material inventory has on Throughput, surfaced a new challenge. The Evaporating Clouds diagram displays this problem clearly.

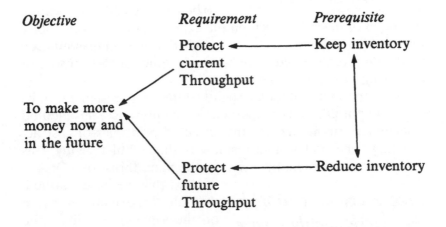

Objective   *Requirement*   *Prerequisite*

Protect ◄——————— Keep inventory
current
Throughput

To make more
money now and
in the future

Protect ◄——————— Reduce inventory
future
Throughput

Rather than wasting time and effort in the attempt to find a "suitable" compromise, all the three methods concentrated on attacking the foundations which gave rise to this conflict. Why is it that we need inventory in order to protect current Throughput? The answer is now very well understood—as long as a system contains both statistical fluctuations and dependent resources, there is a trade-off between Inventory and current Throughput. In previous writing, we showed that even when we start with zero Inventory, Inventory will accumulate to restore Throughput.

No wonder that Total-Quality has been developed by statisticians. If statistical fluctuations are a necessary condition for the need for Inventory, then let's concentrate on reducing statistical fluctuations—or variability as they called it in the attempt to use a more common terminology. No wonder that SPC (Statistical-Process-Control) became a cornerstone technique in TQM. Reduce variability and you reduce the need for maintaining Inventory. The conflict is evaporated without any compromise.

From a global point of view, set-up and breakdowns are just very big fluctuations in process time.

Even a superficial knowledge of JIT is sufficient to recognize that this method also recognizes the same solutions. But since SPC was doing so well in reducing the direct process variability, JIT is more known for its contribution in set-up reduction and preventive maintenance procedures. From a global point of view, set-up and breakdowns are just very big fluctuations in process time.

What is probably less known is the fact that the developers of JIT have concentrated even more on another way to "evaporate" the conflict. Statistical fluctuations are not the only necessary condition creating the need for Inventory, dependent resources is also a necessary condition. So it's no wonder that JIT is so zealous about streamlining the operations. Flow-lines are an excellent way to reduce the amount of resources involved in the production of one product family.

But JIT didn't stop there, it advocates the use of U cell configurations, where one worker is moving with the processed piece from one machine to another. This technique, even though requiring a very big reduction in equipment utilization, drastically reduces the number of dependent resources and thus provides a significant reduction in the level of Inventory needed to protect the current Throughput.

Initially, the Theory of Constraints concentrated on attacking both of the above necessary conditions. Predetermined schedules, reduce both statistical fluctuations and dependent resources. The mere fact that a particular type of resource has, on the average, excess capacity is still far from a guarantee that when a particular part has to be processed by that resource, that it will be instantly available. It might, at that exact moment, be busy processing another part.

Most of the current Inventory does not stem from the need to protect current Throughput, but from erroneous policies.

The reduction in the amount of resources that need to be involved is similar, in effect, to that of the flow lines, (except for the reduction in the resources needed to move the parts from one work center to another, which is more remote) and enables at the same time a much higher machine utilization and flexibility against product mix changes. In effect, the amount of resources involved is restricted, either by physical allocation (flowline) or logical allocation (finite schedule).

As long as the three methods were primarily concerned with their solutions to remove the "inventory conflict," it made a lot of sense to compare them with each other. At that level it's important to try and sort out where they compliment and where a choice has to be made. That was the situation in the early 1980's.

Still, as important and practical as these new solutions may actually be, such contributions certainly do not deserve to be called "new overall management philosophy." First, the application of these solutions is restricted mainly to the factory floor. The factory floor is certainly important, but is it really so much more important than design, distribution, sales or marketing? So much more important that we can use the term "overall"? Second, the changes required are all of mechanical nature; correcting processes to improve quality, rearranging the physical layout and using a different mode of material relies. Is it really justified to refer to such changes as "Management Philosophy?"

Certainly not!

The realization of the need for new overall management philosophies came later. When the effort to reduce inventory has clearly revealed that the current inventory levels do not stem from the need to protect current throughput. The main reasons for their existence and also for the difficulty to reduce them is certainly erroneous policies. That when all three methods have started to preach zealously the . . . absolute obvious.

What can cause TQM to go on barricade preachings ("It's not enough to do things right, we must do the right thing?") unless the wrong things are done on an overwhelming scale?

What can cause JIT to go on the warpath under the banner of "Don't do what is not needed" unless not needed things are done on a grand scale?

What can cause TOC to constantly wave the flag of "The end result of many local optima is certainly not the optimum of the total company," if not for the fact that almost everywhere we are striving to achieve local optima.

The clear vision of the enormity and the magnitude of the trivial mistakes that we are doing stem directly from the fact that these wrong actions are geared to primarily reduce costs.

There is apparently a world of difference between the actions which are required in a "Throughput world" and the one of the "cost world." Such actions which are a must in the "cost world" are regarded as totally devastating when judged through the prism of the "Throughput world."

But where exactly do the methods differ? Not in the judgment of actions, but in the tools/procedures/systems that they offer management to adjust to this entirely different world. JIT is telling us "Don't do what is not needed." Fine, but what is exactly the type of action, the mode of operation, that leads to do things which are not needed? Here JIT stops short.

TQC is warning us to "do the right things"? Fine, what are the guidelines to identify those elusive "right things."? What procedures are we currently using that proclaim us from identifying them? TQC only tells us that to answer this question we must have something mysterious called "profound knowledge."

No wonder that with such ridiculous answers we find ourselves floundering. JIT and TQM certainly open our eyes to the fact that we are living in a different world, the "Throughput world." But they have stopped on its border without providing any map or even a compass. The result today is that it looks like we are no longer satisfied with the excitement of "the end of the month syndrome." We have added to it what can only be called "the beginning of the month project."

Totally exposed to the absolute need to switch gears into the "throughput world" and at the same time not having a clear road map of what it actually is and how to methodically reach it, we just jump from one piece of the puzzle to another. From one worthwhile "project" to another. In this way, the last few years have clearly demonstrated that results are only slowly and painfully achieved. This is definitely not the proper way to join the pieces into a whole.

Only the Theory of Constraint has directly struggled with the global ramifications of putting Throughput to be the number one avenue and tumbling Operating Expenses (cost) from its previous dominant position to the modest stand of being just number three.

What is actually the paradox shift that results from changing the priority scale of the measurements? If Operating Expense is number one, we should consider important every point where operating expense is drained. But Operating Expense is paid in enormous numbers of places. Every worker, engineer, clerk, salesperson, manager, they are all outlets of Operating Expense. As a matter of fact, every consumption of exposable material or consumption of energy is an Operating Expense outlet. The Operating Expense world is a world in which almost everything is important.

Placing Operating Expenses as the dominant measurement causes the impression that our organization is composed of independent variables.

Even if we are led to believe that everything is important, we still remember that some things are more important than others—the Pareto Principle. But as long as operating expenses are considered to be the dominant measurement, the Pareto Principle will be understood as the 20/80 rule. Twenty per cent of the variables are responsible for 80% of the result. This is the case of a system which is composed of independent variables. e.g., the money that we spend on material—80% of the money paid to our vendors is for 20% of our item list, or the money that we get from our clients—80% of the receipts is for 20% of the product list.

No wonder that under this method of running a business, a classification is desperately needed to put some order into the maze of numerous details. The classification used is, of course, the "product cost" which was once totally in line with the dominant concept of operating expense. Managers who work today under that principle will be wrapped in so many details that it is no wonder at all that more than half of their time will be required to put out fires.

But when we make Throughput the dominant factor, the picture drastically changes. In order to achieve a sale many resources have to work in concert for a substantial time. The Throughput is not connected to any one particular action or any particular reason, it achieves only when the actions of many are completed. Putting Throughput as number one forces the realization that our organizations operate as an assemblage of dependent variables.

How much we, as managers, are not prepared to manage using this commonplace undebatable realization, can be easily demonstrated by the fact that most of us really accept the Pareto Principle as the 20/80 rule. In configurations of dependent variables, the Pareto Principle takes the form of 0.1/99.9 rule. Just a fraction of a percent is responsible for almost all the end result. In common practices, unobliterated by fancy sophistication, it was always recognized: "The strength of a chain is only as strong as the weakest link." There are no two "weakest": the number of constraints is very limited and restricted by the number of independent "chains" in our organization.

Of course, switching from 20/80 diffusion into 0.1/99.9 focusing is definitely a "new overall management philosophy." It definitely affects any manager in any type of decision. Not only that it is no longer the prime concern of production-distribution sales or engineering design are not less effected by this concept. The artificial barriers between the functions must be tumbled down. The various functions participate in the same "chains" (products) and thus must consider the impact of a weak link no matter under what function it exists. Managing a part of an organization as if it was an isolated kingdom could have been done as long as operating expense was dominant, but it's impossible to continue when we realize the dominance of Throughput.

It's quite obvious that when the weak links—the constraints— are the ones that determine the end result, they become the main tools of management. The previous tool—product cost— can now be safely discarded. It becomes obsolete when we stop to pay according to piece produced and switch to hourly pay. It becomes devastating when our "overheads" grow to be much larger than direct labor. It's become unnecessary now.

Today when most companies are declaring that jobs will not be lost as a direct result of improvements, it's quite ridiculous to find that they still are using the term "cost reduction programs." If nobody is going to be fired how can cost be reduced? The major reason is, of course, Throughput increased without operating expense increase. The grip of the old concepts is so strong that even the originators of JIT and TQM didn't succeed in actually breaking it.

It's amazing to what extent TQM and JIT have not understood the revolution that they themselves helped to create. In the world of Throughput it is impossible that every quality problem, every set-up reduction, every pile of inventory can possibly be considered as top importance. This way of relating to things is residual of the "cost world." No wonder that the only way to focus the usage of every needed JIT and TQM technique is under their own philosophies which are verbalized only under TOC. It's about time. The diffuse arbitrary way in which we approach the "monthly program" is eroding quickly the good-will of our people.

Some words of caution are needed at this stage. We shouldn't fall into the trap of ever believing that at last we see the ultimate light. We are dealing with management science and science definitely doesn't believe in truth, only in validity. Everything in science is open to question, where truth belongs to the realm of religion. That is why the Theory of Constraints concentrates on the thinking processes, on the verbalization of intuition and regards its applications, not as the ultimate solutions, but at most as powerful ones.

The powerful solutions of today are likely to be the disasters of tomorrow.

Since truth does not exist in science, ultimate solutions do not exist. The highest rank given to a solution is "powerful." When a powerful solution is applied, it changes the entire situation for the better. The bigger the change, the more powerful the solution is. We cannot say given the rank of "powerful solution" to a solution to a relatively unimportant problem. But this change is usually not restricted just to the system, our system does not exist in a vacuum, and thus it also has major ramifications on the environment in which the system operates.

Changes in the environment might require different patterns of behavior from the organization. The important, but unfortunately not broadly recognized, conclusion is that the more powerful the solution, the more probable it is, that it will obsolete itself even faster. If not constantly scrutinized, the powerful solutions of today might turn into our major policy constraints. In a process of ongoing improvement, we can never relax.

What assistance does the Goldratt Institute provide to the Jonahs in their ongoing struggle? Not much, since the Jonahs are supposed to stand on their own two feet, by relying on their own healthy intuition. The relationship is more that of a partnership. Partners in the journey towards generating, exploiting and disseminating the new knowledge.

To assist in this partnership, the Institute provides what it calls the "Jonah-Line." This mechanism is comprised of three major elements:

The first one is access to an external Jonah—an institute associate. These people all have many years of industrial experience and have followed the evolution of the Theory of Constraints through several generations; they are very capable of scrutinizing the implementation plans without criticizing. As was mentioned before, their input is essential to reducing the hidden (but significant) impact of inertia. The associate role is not to assist in constructing the implementation plans and certainly not in helping in the execution of those plans. Their major role is to highlight the negative ramifications of the natural inertia.

This inertia takes two forms. First and foremost is our reluctance to use newly acquired skills. While we felt confident about our abilities in the presence of our teacher, we have many self-doubts when we try to use these skills on our own. Such doubts often become insurmountable hurdles when we try to communicate these techniques to others so we can mutually use them. This is the case with the Effect-Cause-Effect and Evaporating Cloud techniques. The comfort we built up during the Jonah course erodes when we attempt to explain and employ these techniques, especially in the presence of others.

The second form of inertia relates not only to the pursuing of our implementation plan, but also to the "rolling" of it when it is successfully implemented. We tend to forget that a powerful solution changes our environment, necessitating the need for a new, and often different, powerful solution. In *The Goal* Alex Rogo focused his attention on closely managing and scheduling his capacity constraints—heat treat and the NCX-10 machine— and eventually elevated their performance to the point that the real constraint became lack of market demand. Unfortunately, Alex had his own share of inertia and failed to refocus his organization's efforts on exploiting this new constraint. Such an ongoing process is what we call "rolling the implementation plan." We have found that the experience and prodding of an external Jonah is vital to safeguarding against both forms of inertia. This support is provided through periodic visits (typically one day every two months) and telephone access.

The other element of the Jonah Line is a constant updating of the new knowledge generated in the Institute. On a frequent basis, presentations given by the partners of the Institute are video taped. If, as is the usual case, these presentations contain newly developed knowledge, then a synopsis of the video tapes is sent to all the Jonahs (which acquired the Jonah Line) and copies of the appropriate video tapes can be obtained upon request.

The third element is frontal cross fertilization. The mechanism used to accomplish this is the semi-annual Jonah Conference. Twice a year, the Jonahs are getting together for a three day meeting. New situations are raised, experiences are shared and I have the unenviable task of trying to guide and sort out this flood of new knowledge. Because of logistical considerations, the Jonah Conferences for North American and Europe are done separately.

the conference can be appreciated only after one becomes acquainted with the almost exponential rate at which new knowledge is generated.

The immense importance of the conference can be appreciated only after one becomes acquainted with the almost exponential rate at which new knowledge is generated.

Take for example the entire subject of the psychology of the organization and the resulting ramifications it can have on a process of ongoing improvement, which you've read earlier in this book. Almost all this knowledge was verbalized, for the first time, just in the last six months.

APPENDIX

Two Selected Readings from *The Goal*
1. The Encounter
2. The Hike

1

Two weeks ago, I'm wearing the same suit as now. This is back in the good days when I think that everything will work out. I'm traveling, and I'm between planes at O'Hare. I've got some time, so I go to one of the airline lounges. Inside, the place is jammed with business types like me. I'm looking for a seat in this place, gazing over the three-piece pinstripes and the women in conservative blazers and so on, when my eye pauses on the yarmulke worn by the man in the sweater. He's sitting next to a lamp, reading, his book in one hand and his cigar in the other. Next to him there happens to be an empty seat. I make for it. Not until I've almost sat down does it strike me I think I know this guy.

Running into someone you know in the middle of one of the busiest airports in the world carries a shock with it. At first, I'm not sure it's really him. But he looks too much like the physicist I used to know for him to be anyone but Jonah. As I start to sit down, he glances up at me from his book, and I see on his face the same unspoken question: Do I know you?

"Jonah?" I ask him.

"Yes?"

"I'm Alex Rogo. Remember me?"

His face tells me that he doesn't quite.

129

"I knew you some time ago," I tell him. "I was a student. I got a grant to go and study some of the mathematical models you were working on. Remember? I had a beard back then."

A small flash of recognition finally hits him. "Of course! Yes, I do remember you. 'Alex,' was it?"

"Right."

A waitress asks me if I'd like something to drink. I order a scotch and soda and ask Jonah if he'll join me. He decides he'd better not; he has to leave shortly.

"So how are you these days?" I ask.

"Busy," he says. "Very busy. And you?"

"Same here. I'm on my way to Houston right now," I say. "What about you?"

"New York," says Jonah.

He seems a little bored with this line of chit-chat and looks as if he'd like to finish the conversation. A second of quiet falls between us. But, for better or worse, I have this tendency (which I've never been able to bring under control) of filling silence in a conversation with my own voice.

"Funny, but after all those plans I had back then of going into research, I ended up in business," I say. "I'm a plant manager now for UniCo."

Jonah nods. He seems more interested. He takes a puff on his cigar. I keep talking. It doesn't take much to keep me going.

"In fact, that's why I'm on my way to Houston. We belong to a manufacturers' association, and the association invited UniCo to be on a panel to talk about robotics at the annual conference. I got picked by UniCo, because my plant has the most experience with robots."

"I see," says Jonah. "Is this going to be a technical discussion?"

"More business oriented than technical," I say. Then I remember I have something I can show him. "Wait a second. . . ."

I crack open my briefcase on my lap and pull out the advance copy of the program the association sent me.

"Here we are," I say, and read the listing to him. " 'Robotics:

Solution for the Eighties to America's Productivity Crisis . . . a panel of users and experts discusses the coming impact of industrial robots on American manufacturing.' "

But when I look back to him, Jonah doesn't seem very impressed. I figure, well, he's an academic person; he's not going to understand the business world.

"You say your plant uses robots?" he asks.

"In a couple of departments, yes," I say.

"Have they really increased productivity at your plant?"

"Sure they have," I say. "We had—what?" I scan the ceiling for the figure. "I think it was a thirty-six percent improvement in one area."

"Really . . . thirty-six percent?" asks Jonah. "So your company is making thirty-six percent more money from your plant just from installing some robots? Incredible."

I can't hold back a smile.

"Well . . . no," I say. "We all wish it were that easy! But it's a lot more complicated than that. See, it was just in one department that we had a thirty-six percent improvement."

Jonah looks at his cigar, then extinguishes it in the ashtray.

"Then you didn't really increase productivity," he says.

I feel my smile freeze.

"I'm not sure I understand," I say.

Jonah leans forward conspiratorially and says, "Let me ask you something—just between us: Was your plant able to ship even one more product per day as a result of what happened in the department where you installed the robots?"

I mumble, "Well, I'd have to check the numbers . . ."

"Did you fire anybody?" he asks.

I lean back, looking at him. What the hell does he mean by that?

"You mean did we lay anybody off? Because we installed the robots?" I say. "No, we have an understanding with our union that nobody will be laid off because of productivity improvement. We shifted the people to other jobs. Of course, when there's a business downturn, we lay people off."

"But the robots themselves didn't reduce your plant's people expense," he says.

"No," I admit.

"Then, tell me, did your inventories go down?" asks Jonah. I chuckle.

"Hey, Jonah, what is this?" I say to him.

"Just tell me," he says. "Did inventories go down?"

"Offhand, I have to say I don't think so. But I'd really have to check the numbers."

"Check your numbers if you'd like," says Jonah. "But if your inventories haven't gone down . . . and your employee expense was not reduced . . . and if your company isn't selling more products—which obviously it can't, if you're not shipping more of them—then you can't tell me these robots increased your plant's productivity."

In the pit of my stomach, I'm getting this feeling like you'd probably have if you were in an elevator and the cable snapped.

"Yeah, I see what you're saying, in a way," I tell him. "But my efficiencies went up, my costs went down—"

"Did they?" asks Jonah. He closes his book.

"Sure they did. In fact, those efficiencies are averaging well above ninety percent. And my cost per part went down considerably. Let me tell you, to stay competitive these days, we've got to do everything we can to be more efficient and reduce costs."

My drink arrives; the waitress puts it on the table beside me. I hand her a five and wait for her to give me the change.

"With such high efficiencies, you must be running your robots constantly," says Jonah.

"Absolutely," I tell him. "We have to. Otherwise, we'd lose our savings on our cost per part. And efficiencies would go down. That applies not only to the robots, but to our other production resources as well. We have to keep producing to stay efficient and maintain our cost advantage."

"Really?" he says.

"Sure. Of course, that's not to say we don't have our problems."

"I see," says Jonah. Then he smiles. "Come on! Be honest. Your inventories are going through the roof, are they not?"

I look at him. How does he know?

"If you mean our work-in-process—"

"All of your inventories," he says.

"Well, it depends. Some places, yes, they are high," I say.

"And everything is always late?" asks Jonah. "You can't ship anything on time?"

"One thing I'll admit," I tell him, "is that we have a heck of a problem meeting shipping dates. It's a serious issue with customers lately."

Jonah nods, as if he had predicted it.

"Wait a minute here . . . how come you know about these things?" I ask him.

He smiles again.

"Just a hunch," says Jonah. "Besides, I see those symptoms in a lot of the manufacturing plants. You're not alone."

I say, "But aren't you a physicist?"

"I'm a scientist," he says "And right now you could say I'm doing work in the science of organizations—manufacturing organizations in particular."

"Didn't know there was such a science."

"There is now," he says.

"Whatever it is you're into, you put your finger on a couple of my biggest problems, I have to give you that," I tell him. "How come—"

I stop because Jonah is exclaiming something in Hebrew He's reached into a pocket of his trousers to take out an old watch. "Sorry, Alex, but I see I'm going to miss my plane if I don't hurry," he says.

He stands up and reaches for his coat.

"That's too bad," I say. "I'm kind of intrigued by a couple of things you've said."

Jonah pauses.

"Yes, well, if you could start to think about what we've been discussing, you probably could get your plant out of the trouble it's in."

"Hey, maybe I gave you the wrong impression," I tell him. "We've got a few problems, but I wouldn't say the plant is in *trouble.*"

He looks me straight in the eye. He knows what's going on, I'm thinking.

"But tell you what," I hear myself saying, "I've got some time to kill. Why don't I walk you down to your plane? Would you mind?"

"No, not at all," he says. "But we have to hurry."

I get up and grab my coat and briefcase. My drink is sitting there. I take a quick slurp off the top and abandon it. Jonah is already edging his way toward the door. He waits for me to catch up with him. Then the two of us step out into the corridor where people are rushing everywhere. Jonah sets off at a fast pace. It takes an effort to keep up with him.

"I'm curious," I tell Jonah, "what made you suspect something might be wrong with my plant?"

"You told me yourself," Jonah says.

"No, I didn't."

"Alex," he says, "it was clear to me from your own words that you're not running as efficient a plant as you think you are. You are running exactly the opposite. You are running a very *in*efficient plant."

"Not according to the measurements," I tell him. "Are you trying to tell me my people are wrong in what they're reporting . . . that they're lying to me or something?"

"No," he says. "It is very unlikely your people are lying to you. But your measurements definitely are."

"Yeah, okay, sometimes we massage the numbers here and there. But everybody has to play that game."

"You're missing the point," he says. "You *think* you're running an efficient plant . . . but your thinking is wrong."

"What's wrong with my thinking? It's no different from the thinking of most other managers."

"Yes, exactly," says Jonah.

"What's that supposed to mean?" I ask; I'm beginning to feel somewhat insulted by this.

"Alex, if you're like nearly everybody else in this world, you've accepted so many things without question that you're not really thinking at all," says Jonah.

"Jonah, I'm thinking all the time," I tell him. "That's part of my job."

He shakes his head.

"Alex, tell me again why you believe your robots are such a great improvement."

"Because they increased productivity," I say.

"And what is productivity?"

I think for a minute, try to remember.

"According to the way my company is defining it," I tell him, "there's a formula you use, something about the value added per employee equals. . . ."

Jonah is shaking his head again.

"Regardless of how your company defines it, that is not what productivity really is," he says. "Forget for just a minute about the formulas and all that, and just tell me in your own words, from your own experience, what does it mean to be productive?"

We rush around a corner. In front of us, I see, are the metal detectors and the security guards. I had intended to stop and say good-bye to him here, but Jonah doesn't slow down.

"Just tell me, what does it mean to be productive?" he asks again as he walks through the metal detector. From the other side he talks to me. "To *you* personally, what does it mean?"

I put my briefcase on the conveyor and follow him through. I'm wondering, what does he want to hear?

On the far side, I'm telling him, "Well, I guess it means that I'm accomplishing something."

"Exactly!" he says. "But you are accomplishing something in terms of what?"

"In terms of my goals," I say.

"Correct!" says Jonah.

He reaches under his sweater into his shirt pocket and pulls out a cigar. He hands it to me.

"My compliments," he says. "When you are productive you are accomplishing something in terms of your goal, right?"

"Right," I say as I retrieve my briefcase.

We're rushing past gate after gate. I'm trying to match Jonah stride for stride.

And he's saying, "Alex, I have come to the conclusion that productivity is the act of bringing a company closer to its goal. Every action that brings a company closer to its goal is productive. Every action that does not bring a company closer to its goal is not productive. Do you follow me?"

"Yeah, but . . . really, Jonah, that's just simple common sense," I say to him.

"It's simple logic is what it is," he says.

We stop. I watch him hand his ticket across the counter.

"But it's too simplified," I tell him. "It doesn't tell me anything. I mean, if I'm moving toward my goal I'm productive and if I'm not, then I'm not productive—so what?"

"What I'm telling you is, productivity is meaningless unless you know what your goal is," he says.

He takes his ticket and starts to walk toward the gate.

"Okay, then," I say. "You can look at it this way. One of my company's goals is to increase efficiencies. Therefore, whenever I increase efficiencies, I'm being productive. It's logical."

Jonah stops dead. He turns to me.

"Do you know what your problem is?" he asks me.

"Sure," I say. "I need better efficiencies."

"No, that is not your problem," he says. "Your problem is you don't know what the goal is. And, by the way, there is only one goal, no matter what the company."

That stumps me for a second. Jonah starts walking toward the gate again. It seems everyone else has now gone on board. Only the two of us are left in the waiting area. I keep after him.

"Wait a minute! What do you mean, I don't know what the goal is? I know what the goal is," I tell him.

By now, we're at the door of the plane. Jonah turns to me. The stewardess inside the cabin is looking at us.

"Really? Then, tell me, what is the goal of your manufacturing organization?" he asks.

"The goal is to produce products as efficiently as we can," I tell him.

"Wrong," says Jonah. "That's not it. What is the real goal?"

I stare at him blankly.

The stewardess leans through the door.

"Are either of you going to board this aircraft?"

Jonah says to her, "Just a second, please." Then he turns to me. "Come on, Alex! Quickly! Tell me the real goal, if you know what it is."

"Power?" I suggest.

He looks surprised. "Well . . . not bad, Alex. But you don't get power just by virtue of manufacturing something."

The stewardess is pissed off. "Sir, if you're not getting on this aircraft, you have to go back to the terminal," she says coldly.

Jonah ignores her. "Alex, you cannot understand the meaning of productivity unless you know what the goal is. Until then, you're just playing a lot of games with numbers and words."

"Okay, then it's market share," I tell him. "That's the goal."

"Is it?" he asks.

He steps into the plane.

"Hey! Can't you tell me?" I call to him.

"Think about it, Alex. You can find the answer with your own mind," he says.

He hands the stewardess his ticket, looks at me and waves good-bye. I raise my hand to wave back and discover I'm still holding the cigar he gave me. I put it in my suit jacket pocket. When I look up again, he's gone. An impatient gate-agent appears and tells me flatly she is going to close the door.

2

I open my eyes Saturday morning to see a drab green blur. The blur turns out to be my son, Dave, dressed in his Boy Scout uniform. He is shaking my arm.

"Davey, what are you doing here?" I ask.

He says, "Dad, it's seven o'clock!"

"Seven o'clock? I'm trying to sleep. Aren't you supposed to be watching television or something?"

"We'll be late," he says.

"We will be late? For what?"

"For the overnight hike!" he says. "Remember? You promised me I could volunteer you to go along and help the troopmaster."

I mutter something no Boy Scout should ever hear. But Dave isn't fazed.

"Come on. Just get in the shower," he says, as he pulls me out of bed. "I packed your gear last night. Everything's in the car already. We just have to get there by eight."

I manage a last look at Julie, her eyes still shut, and the warm soft mattress as Davey drags me through the door.

An hour and ten minutes later, my son and I arrive at the edge of some forest. Waiting for us is the troop: fifteen boys outfitted in caps, neckerchiefs, merit badges, the works.

Before I have time to say, "Where's the troopmaster?", the other few parents who happen to be lingering with the boys take off in their cars, all pedals to the metal. Looking around, I see that I am the only adult in sight.

"Our troopmaster couldn't make it," says one of the boys.

"How come?"

"He's sick," says another kid next to him.

"Yeah, his hemorrhoids are acting up," says the first. "So it looks like you're in charge now."

"What are we supposed to do, Mr. Rogo?" asks the other kid.

Well, at first I'm a little mad at having all this foisted upon me. But then the idea of having to supervise a bunch of kids doesn't daunt me—after all, I do that every day at the plant. So I gather everyone around. We look at a map and discuss the objectives for this expedition into the perilous wilderness before us.

The plan, I learn, is for the troop to hike through the forest following a blazed trail to someplace called "Devil's Gulch." There we are to bivouac for the evening. In the morning we are to break camp and make our way back to the point of departure, where Mom and Dad are supposed to be waiting for little Freddy and Johnny and friends to walk out of the woods.

First, we have to get to Devil's Gulch, which happens to be about ten miles away. So I line up the troop. They've all got their rucksacks on their backs. Map in hand, I put myself at front of the line in order to lead the way, and off we go.

The weather is fantastic. The sun is shining through the trees. The skies are blue. It's breezy and the temperature is a little on the cool side, but once we get into the woods, it's just right for walking.

The trail is easy to follow because there are blazes (splotches of yellow paint) on the tree trunks every 10 yards or so. On either side, the undergrowth is thick. We have to hike in single file. So I wait for the first boy to catch up to me, and I ask him his name.

"I'm Ron," he says.

"Ron, I want you to lead the column," I tell him, handing

over the map. "Just keep following this trail, and set a moderate pace. Okay?"

"Right, Mr. Rogo."

And he sets off at what seems to be a reasonable pace.

"Everybody stay behind Ron!" I call back to the others. "Nobody passes Ron, because he's got the map. Understand?"

Everybody nods, waves. Everybody understands.

I wait by the side of the trail as the troop passes. Five or six boys come along, all of them keeping up without any problems. Then there is a gap, followed by a couple more scouts. After them, another, even larger gap has occured. I look down the trail. And I see this fat kid named Herbie. Behind him is the rest of the troop.

Herbie continues up the trail and the others follow. Some of them look as if they'd like to go faster, but they can't get around Herbie. I fall in behind the last boy. The line stretches out in front of me, and most of the time, unless we're going over a hill of around a sharp bend in the trail, I can see everybody. The column seems to settle into a comfortable rhythm.

I start thinking about the conversation I had with Jonah in New York.

Obviously we have dependent events in manufacturing. All it means is that one operation has to be done before a second operation can be performed. Parts are made in sequence of steps. Machine a has to finish Step One before Worker B can proceed with Step Two. All the parts have to be finished before we can assemble the product. The product has to be assembled before we can ship it. And so on.

But you find dependent events in any process, and not just those in a factory. Driving a car requires a sequence of dependent events. So does the hike we're taking now. In order to arrive at Devil's Gulch, a trail has to be walked. Up front, Ron has to walk the trail before Davey can walk it. Davey has to walk the trail before Herbie can walk it. In order for me to walk the trail, the boy in front of me has to walk it first. It's a simple case of dependent events.

And statistical fluctuations?

I look up and notice that the boy in front of me is going a little faster than I have been. He's a few feet farther ahead of me than he was a minute ago. So I take some bigger steps to catch up. Then, for a second, I'm too close to him, so I slow down.

There: if I'd been measuring my stride, I would have recorded statistical fluctuations. But, again, what's the big deal?

If I say that I'm walking at the rate of "two miles per hour," I don't mean I'm walking exactly at a constant rate of two miles per hour every instant. Sometimes I'll be going 2.5 miles per hour; sometimes maybe I'll be walking at only 1.2 miles per hour. The rate is going to fluctuate according to the length and speed of each step. But over time and distance, I should be *averaging* about two miles per hour, more or less.

The same thing happens in the plant. How long does it take to solder the wire leads on a transformer? Well, if you get out your stopwatch and time the operation over and over again, you might find that it takes, let's say, 4.3 minutes on the average. But the actual time on any given instance may range between 2.1 minutes up to 6.4 minutes. And nobody in advance can say, "This one will take 2.1 minutes . . . this one will take 5.8 minutes." Nobody can predict that information.

So what's wrong with that? Nothing as far as I can see. Anyway, we don't have any choice. What else are we going to use in place of an "average" or an "estimate"?

I find I'm almost stepping on the boy in front of me. We've slowed down somewhat. It's because we're climbing a long, fairly steep hill. All of us are backed up behind Herbie.

Then Herbie reaches the top. He turns around. His face is red from the climb.

"Atta boy, Herbie!" I say to encourage him. "Let's keep it moving!"

Herbie disappears over the crest. The others continue the climb, and I trudge behind them until I get to the top. Pausing there, I look down the trail.

Ron must be a half a mile ahead of us. I can see a couple of boys in front of Herbie, and everyone else is lost in the distance. I cup my hands over my mouth.

"HEY! LET'S GO UP THERE! LET'S CLOSE RANKS!" I yell. "DOUBLE TIME! DOUBLE TIME!"

Herbie eases into a trot. After a couple hundred yards, we still haven't caught up. Herbie is slowing down. Finally I see Ron off in the distance.

"HEY RON!" I shout. "HOLD UP!"

The call is relayed up the trail by the other boys. Herbie slows to a fast walk. And so do the rest of us.

"Ron, I thought I told you to set a moderate pace," I say.

"But I did!" he protests.

"Okay, let's take a break," I tell them.

According to the map we have only gone about two miles.

"All right, let's go," I say.

We start out again. The trail is straight here, so I can see everyone. We haven't gone thirty yards before I notice it starting all over again. The line is spreading out; gaps between the boys are widening. Dammit, we're going to be running and stopping all day long if this keeps up. Half the troop is liable to get lost if we can't stay together.

I've got to put an end to this.

The first one I check is Ron. But Ron, indeed, is setting a steady, "average" pace for the troop—a pace nobody should have any trouble with. I look back down the line, and all of the boys are walking at about the same rate as Ron. And Herbie? He's not the problem anymore. Maybe he felt responsible for the last delay, because now he seems to be making a special effort to keep up. He's right on the ass of the kid in front of him.

If we're all walking at about the same pace, why is the distance between Ron, at the front of the line, and me, at the end of the line, increasing?

Statistical fluctuations?

Nah, couldn't be. The fluctuations should be averaging out. We're all moving at about the same speed, so that should mean the distance between any of us will vary somewhat, but will even out over a period of time. The distance between Ron and me should also expand and contract within a certain range, but should average about the same throughout the hike.

But it isn't. As long as each of us is maintaining a normal, moderate pace like Ron, the length of the column is increasing. The gaps between us are expanding.

Except between Herbie and the kid in front of him.

So how is he doing it? I watch him. Every time Herbie gets a step behind, he runs for an extra step. Which means he's actually expending more energy than Ron or the others at the front of the line in order to maintain the same relative speed. I'm wondering how long he'll be able to keep up his walk-run routine.

Yet . . . why can't we all just walk at the same pace as Ron and stay together?

I'm watching the line when something up ahead catches my eye. I see Davey slow down for a few seconds. He's adjusting his packstraps. In front of him, Ron continues onward, oblivious. A gap of ten . . . fifteen . . . twenty feet opens up. Which means the entire line has grown by 20 feet.

That's when I begin to understand what's happening.

Ron is setting the pace. Every time someone moves slower than Ron, the line lengthens. It wouldn't even have to be as obvious as when Dave slowed down. If one of the boys takes a step that's half an inch shorter than the one Ron took, the length of the whole line could be affected.

But what happens when someone moves faster than Ron? Aren't the longer or faster steps supposed to make up for the spreading? Don't the differences average out?

Suppose I walk faster. Can I shorten the length of the line? Well, between me and the kid ahead of me is a gap of about five feet. If he continues walking at the same rate, and if I speed up, I can reduce the gap—and maybe reduce the total length of the column, depending upon what's happening up ahead. But I can only do that until I'm bumping the kid's rucksack. So I have to slow down to his rate.

Once I've closed the gap between us, I can't go any faster than the rate at which the kid in front of me is going. And he ultimately can't go any faster than the kid in front of him. And so on up the line to Ron. Which means that, except for Ron, each of our speeds depends upon the speeds of those in front of us in the line.

It's starting to make sense. Our hike is a set of dependent events . . . in combination with statistical fluctuations. Each of us is fluctuating in speed, faster and slower. But the ability to go faster than average is restricted. It depends upon all the others ahead of me in the line. So even if I could walk five miles per hour, I couldn't do it if the boy in front of me could only walk two miles per hour. And even if the kid directly in front of me could walk that fast, neither of us could do it unless all the boys in the line were moving at five miles per hour at the same time.

So I've got limits on how fast I can go—both my own (I can only go so fast for so long before I fall over and pant to death) and those of the others on the hike. However, there is no limit on my ability to slow down. Or on anyone else's ability to slow down. Or stop. And if any of us did, the line would extend indefinitely.

What's happening isn't an averaging out of the fluctuations in our various speeds, but an *accumulation* of the fluctuations. And mostly it's an accumulation of slowness—*because dependency limits the opportunities for higher fluctuations.* And that's why the line is spreading. We can make the line shrink only by having everyone in the back of the line move much faster than Ron's average over some distance.

Looking ahead, I can see that how much distance each of us has to make up tends to be a matter of where we are in the line. Davey only has to make up for his own slower than average fluctuations relative to Ron—that twenty feet or so which is the gap in front of him. But for Herbie to keep the length of the line from growing, he would have to make up for his own fluctuations plus those of all the kids in front of him. And here I am at the end of the line. To make the total length of the line contract, I have to move faster than average for a distance equal to all the excess space between all the boys. I have to make up for the accumulation of all their slowness.

Then I start to wonder what this could mean to me on the job. In the plant, we've definitely got both dependent events and statistical fluctuations. And here on the trail we've got both of them. What if I were to say that this troop of boys is analogous to a manufacturing system . . . sort of a model. In fact, the troop does produce a product; we produce "walk trail." Ron begins production by consuming the unwalked trail before him, which is the equivalent of raw materials. So Ron processes the trail first by walking over it, then Davey has to process it next, followed by the boy behind him, and so on back to Herbie and the others and on to me.

Each of us is like an operation which has to be performed to produce a product in the plant; each of us is one of a set of dependent events. Does it matter what order we're in? Well, somebody has to be first and somebody else has to be last. So we have dependent events no matter if we switch the order of the boys.

I'm the last operation. Only after I have walked the trail is the product "sold," so to speak. And that would have to be our throughput—not the rate at which Ron walks the trail, but the rate at which I do.

What about the amount of trail between Ron and me? It has to be inventory. Ron is consuming raw materials, so the trail the rest of us are walking is inventory until it passes behind me.

And what is operational expense? It's whatever lets us turn inventory into throughput, which in our case would be the energy the boys need to walk. I can't really quantify that for the model, except that I know when I'm getting tired.

If the distance between Ron and me is expanding, it can only mean that inventory is increasing. Throughput is my rate of walking. Which is influenced by the fluctuating rates of the others. Hmmm. So as the slower than average fluctuations accumulate, they work their way back to me. Which means I have to slow down. Which means that, relative to the growth of inventory, throughput for the entire system goes down.

And operational expense? I'm not sure. For UniCo, whenever inventory goes up, carrying costs on the inventory go up as well.

Carrying costs are a part of operational expense, so that measurement also must be going up. In terms of the hike, operational expense is increasing any time we hurry to catch up, because we expend more energy than we otherwise would.

Inventory is going up. Throughput is going down. And operational expense is probably increasing.

Is that what's happening in my plant?

Yes, I think it is.

Just then, I look up and see that I'm nearly running into the kid in front of me.

Ah ha! Okay! Here's proof I must have overlooked something in the analogy. The line in front of me is contracting rather than expanding. Everything must be averaging out after all. I'm going to lean to the side and see Ron walking his average two-mile-an-hour pace.

But Ron is not walking the average pace. He's standing still at the edge of the trail.

"How come we're stopping?"

He says, "Time for lunch, Mr. Rogo."

I sit down at one of the tables and ponder a few thoughts as I eat a sandwich. What's bothering me now is that, first of all, there is no real way I could operate a manufacturing plant without having dependent events and statistical fluctuations. I can't get away from that combination. But there must be a way to overcome the effects. I mean, obviously, we'd all go out of business if inventory was always increasing, and throughput was always decreasing.

If I could get capacity perfectly balanced with demand, wouldn't my excess inventory go away? Wouldn't my shortages of certain parts disappear? Managers have always trimmed capacity to cut costs and increase profits; that's the game.

I'm beginning to think maybe this hiking model has thrown me off. I mean, sure, it shows me the effect of statistical fluctuations and dependent events in combination. But is it a balanced system? Let's say the demand on us is to walk two miles every hour—no more, no less. Could I adjust the capacity of each kid so he would be able to walk two miles per hour and no faster? If

I could, I'd simply keep everyone moving constantly at the pace he should go—by yelling, whip-cracking, money, whatever—and everything would be perfectly balanced.

The problem is how can I realistically trim the capacity of fifteen kids?

I'm puzzling over how to do this when I notice a kid sitting at one of the tables, rolling a pair of dice.

"Say, mind if I borrow those for a while?" I ask.

The kid shrugs, then hands them over.

I go back to the table again and roll the dice a couple of times. Yes, indeed: statistical fluctuations. Every time I roll the dice, I get a random number that is predictable only within a certain range, specifically numbers one to six on each die. Now what I need next for the model is a set of dependent events.

After scavenging around for a minute or two, I find a box of match sticks (the strike-anywhere kind), and some bowls from the aluminum mess kit. I set the bowls in a line along the length of the table and put the matches a tone end. And this gives me a model of a perfectly balanced system.

While I'm setting this up and figuring out how to operate the model, Dave wanders over with a friend of his. They stand by the table and watch me roll the die and move the matches around.

"What are you doing?" asks Dave.

"Well, I'm sort of inventing a game," I say.

"A game? Really?" says his friend. "Can we play it, Mr. Rogo?"

Why not?

"Sure you can," I say.

All of a sudden Dave is interested.

"Hey, can I play too?" he asks.

"Yeah, I guess I'll let you in," I tell him. "In fact, why don't you round up a couple more of the guys to help us do this."

While they go get the others, I figure out the details. The system I've set up is intended to "process" matches. It does this by moving a quantity of match sticks out of their box, and through each of the bowls in succession. The dice determine how many matches can be moved from one bowl to the next. The dice represent the capacity of each resource, each bowl; the set of bowls are my dependent events, my stages of production. Each has exactly the same capacity as the others, but its actual yield will fluctuate somewhat.

In order to keep those fluctuations minimal, however, I decide to use only one of the dice. This allows the fluctuations to range from one to six. So from the first bowl, I can move to the next bowls in line any quantity of matches ranging from a minimum of one to a maximum of six.

Throughput in this system is the speed at which matches come out of the last bowl. Inventory consists of the total number of matches in all of the bowls at any time. And I'm going to assume that market demand is exactly equal to the average number of matches that the system can process. Production capacity of each resource and market demand are perfectly in balance. So that means I now have a model of a perfectly balanced manufacturing plant.

Five of the boys decide to play. Besides Dave, there are Andy, Ben, Chuck, and Evan. Each of them sits behind one of the bowls. I find some paper and a pencil to record what happens. Then I explain what they're supposed to do.

"The idea is to move as many matches as you can from your bowl to the bowl on your left. When it's your turn, you roll the die, and the number that comes up is the number of matches you can move. Got it?"

They all nod. "But you can only move as many matches as you've got in your bowl. So if you roll a five and you only have two matches in your bowl, then you can only move two matches. And if it comes to your turn and you don't have any matches, then naturally you can't move any."

They nod again.

"How many matches do you think we can move through the line each time we go through the cycle?" I ask them.

Perplexity descends over their faces.

"Well, if you're able to move a maximum of six and a minimum of one when it's your turn, what's the average number you ought to be moving?" I ask them.

"Three," says Andy.

"No, it won't be three," I tell them. "The mid-point between one and six isn't three."

I draw some numbers on my paper.

"Here, look," I say, and I show them this:

1 2 3 4 5 6

And I explain that 3.5 is really the average of those six numbers.

"So how many matches do you think each of you should have moved on the average after we've gone through the cycle a number of times?" I ask.

"Three and a half per turn," says Andy.

"And after ten cycles?"

"Thirty-five," says Chuck.

"And after twenty cycles?"

"Seventy," says Ben.

"Okay, let's see if we can do it," I say.

Then I hear a long sigh from the end of the table. Evan looks at me.

"Would you mind if I don't play this game, Mr. Rogo?" he asks.

"How come?"

"'Cause I think it's going to be kind of boring," he says.

"Yeah," says Chuck. "Just moving matches around. Like who cares, you know?"

"I think I'd rather go tie some knots," says Evan.

"Tell you what," I say. "Just to make it more interesting, we'll have a reward. Let's say that everybody has a quota of 3.5 matches per turn. Anybody who does better than that, who averages more than 3.5 matches, doesn't have to wash any dishes tonight. But anybody who averages less than 3.5 per turn, has to do extra dishes after dinner."

"Yeah, all right!" says Evan.

"You got it!" says Dave.

They're all excited now. They're practicing rolling the die.

Meanwhile, I set up a grid on a sheet of paper. What I plan to do is record the amount that each of them deviates from the average. They all start at zero. If the roll of the die is a 4, 5, or 6 then I'll record—respectively—a gain of .5, 1.5, or 2.5. And if the roll is a 1, 2, or 3 then I'll record a loss of −.5, −1.5 or −2.5 respectively. The deviations, of course, have to be cumulative; if someone is 2.5 above, for example, his starting point on the next turn is 2.5, not zero. That's the way it would happen in the plant.

"Okay, everybody ready?" I ask.

"All set."

I give the die to Andy.

He rolls a two. So he takes two matches from the box and puts them in Ben's bowl. By rolling a two, Andy is down 1.5 from his quota of 3.5 and I note the deviation on the chart.

Ben rolls next and the die comes up as a four.

Ben passes his two matches to Chuck. I record a deviation of −1.5 for him too.

Chuck rolls next. He gets a five. But, again, there are only two matches he can move.

Chuck passes his measly two matches down to Dave, and I record a deviation of −1.5 for Chuck as well. We watch as Dave rolls the die. His roll is only one. He takes the one match out of his bowl and puts it on the end of the table. For both Dave and Evan, I wrote a deviation of −2.5.

"Okay, let's see if we can do better next time," I say.

Andy shakes the die in his hand for what seems like an hour. The die goes spinning onto the table. We all look. It's a six.

"All right!"

"Way to go, Andy!"

He takes six match sticks out of the box and hands them to Ben. I record a gain of +2.5 for him, which puts his score at 1.0 on the grid.

Ben takes the die and he too rolls a six. More cheers. He passes all six matches to Chuck. I record the same score for Ben as for Andy.

But Chuck rolls a three. So after he passes three matches to

Dave, he still has three left in his bowl. And I note a loss of −0.5 on the chart.

Now Dave rolls the die; it comes up as a six. But he only has four matches to pass—the three that Chuck just passed to him and one from the last round. So he passes four to Evan. I write down a gain of +0.5 for him.

Evan gets a three on the die. So the lone match on the end of the table is joined by three more. Evan still has one left in his bowl. And I record a loss of −0.5 for Evan.

At the end of two rounds, this is what the chart looks like.

	ANDY	BEN	CHUCK	DAVE	EVAN
Turn:	1234567890	1234567890	1234567890	1234567890	1234567890
Roll - - - - -	26	46	43	16	13
#Moved	26	26	23	14	13
Inventory:		00	03	10	01
Change +/−					
+2					
+1.5					
+1	*	*			
+0.5					
0					
−1					
−1.5	*	*	*		
−2			*	*	
−2.5				*	*
−3					*
−3.5					

We keep going. The die spins on the table and passes from hand to hand. Matches come out of the box and move from bowl to bowl. Andy's rolls are—what else?—very average, no steady run of high or low numbers. He is able to meet the quota and then some. At the other end of the table, it's a different story.

"Hey, let's keep those matches coming."

"Yeah, we need more down here."

"Keep rolling sixes, Andy."

Eliyahu M. Goldratt

"It isn't Andy, it's Chuck. Look at him, he's got five."

After four turns, I have to add more numbers—negative numbers—to the bottom of the chart. Not for Andy or for Ben or for Chuck, but for Dave and Evan. For them, it looks like there is no bottom deep enough.

After five rounds, the chart looks like this:

	ANDY	BEN	CHUCK	DAVE	EVAN
Turn:	1234567890	1234567890	1234567890	1234567890	1234567890
Roll - - - - -	26425	46152	43225	16351	13641
#Moved	26452	26152	23225	14221	13321
Inventory:		00303	03252	10004	01000

```
Change +/-
+2.5
+2
+1.5          * *
+1          *           *
+0.5
  0 ---------*--------*--------------------------------
-0.5               *
-1
-1.5      *        * *
-2                     *            *
-2.5                                *             *
-3                                                  *
-3.5                          * *          *
-4                                                    *
-4.5
-5                            *          *
-5.5                                                 *
-6
-6.5
-7
-7.5                                        *
-8                                                    *
-8.5
```

"How am I doing, Mr. Rogo?" Evan asks me.

"Well, Evan . . . ever hear the story of the Titanic?"

He looks depressed.

"You've got five rounds left," I tell him. "Maybe you can pull through."

"Yeah, remember the law of averages," says Chuck.

"If I have to wash dishes because you guys didn't give me enough matches . . ." says Evan, letting vague implications of threat hang in the air.

"I'm doing my job up here," says Andy.

"Yeah, what's wrong with you guys down there?" asks Ben.

"Hey, I just now got enough of them to pass," says Dave. "I've hardly had any before."

Indeed, some of the inventory which had been stuck in the first three bowls had finally moved to Dave. But now it gets stuck in Dave's bowl. The couple of higher rolls he had in the first five rounds are averaging out. Now he's getting low rolls just when he has inventory to move.

"C'mon, Dave, gimme some matches," says Evan.

Dave rolls a one.

"Aw, Dave! One match!"

"Andy, you hear what we're having for dinner tonight?" asks Ben.

"I think it's spaghetti," says Andy.

"Ah, man, that'll be a mess to clean up."

"Yeah, glad I won't have to do it," says Andy.

"You just wait," says Evan. "You just wait 'til Dave gets some good numbers for a change."

But it doesn't get any better.

"How are we doing now, Mr. Rogo?" asks Evan.

"I think there's a Brillo pad with your name on it."

"All right! No dishes tonight!" shouts Andy.

After ten rounds, this is how the chart looks . . . (see next page)

I look at the chart. I still can hardly believe it. It was a balanced system. And yet throughput went down. Inventory went up. And operational expense? If there had been carrying costs on the matches, operational expense would have gone up too.

What if this had been a real plant—with real customers? How many units did we manage to ship? We expected to ship thirty-five. But what was our actual throughput? It was only twenty. About half of what we needed. And it was nowhere near the maximum potential of each station. If this had been an actual plant, half of our orders—or more—would have been late. We'd never be able to promise specific delivery dates. And if we did, our credibility with customers would drop through the floor.

	ANDY	BEN	CHUCK	DAVE	EVAN
Turn:	1234567890	1234567890	1234567890	1234567890	1234567890
Roll - - - - -	2642536452	4615254633	4322561565	1635122132	1364145342
#Moved	2642536452	2615254633	2422561565	1422122132	1332122132
Inventory:		0030313132	0325214510	1000487###	0100000000

```
Change +/-
+5.5              *
+5
+4.5                      *
+4          * *           *
+3.5          *           *
+3
+2.5
+2                  *           *
+1.5      * *         *
+1      *   *       *
+0.5
  0 - - - - - - * - - - - - * - - - - - - - - - - - - - - - - - -
-0.5              *
-1                              *
-1.5    *       * *         *
-2                  *       *       *
-2.5                              *       *
-3                                        *
-3.5              * * *         *
-4                                        *
-4.5
-5                      *           *
-5.5                                        *
-6
-6.5
-7
-7.5                              *
-8                                        *
-8.5
-9                                  *
-9.5                                        *
-10
-10.5                             *
-11
-11.5                                       *
```

```
-12
-12.5
-13                                              *
-13.5                                      *          *
-14                                                      *
-14.5                                 *
-15
-15.5                                                      *
```

\# Dave's inventory for turns 8, 9, and 10 is in double digits, respectively rising to 11 matches, 14 matches, and 17 matches.

All of that sounds familiar, doesn't it?

"Hey, we can't stop now!" Evan is clamoring.

"Yea, let's keep playing," says Dave.

"Okay," says Andy. "What do you want to bet this time? I'll take you on."

"Let's play for who cooks dinner," says Ben.

"Great," says Dave.

"You're on," says Evan.

They roll the die for another twenty rounds, but I run out of paper at the bottom of the page while tracking Dave and Evan. What was I expecting? My initial chart ranged from +6 to −6. I guess I was expecting some fairly regular highs and lows, a normal sine curve. But I didn't get that. Instead, the chart looks like I'm tracing a cross-section of the Grand Canyon. Inventory moves through the system not in manageable flow, but in waves. The mound of matches in Dave's bowl passes to Evan's and onto the table finally—only to be replaced by another accumulating wave. And the system gets further and further behind schedule.

"Want to play again?" asks Andy.

"Yeah, only this time I get your seat," says Evan.

"No way!" says Andy.

Chuck is in the middle shaking his head, already resigned to defeat. Anyway, it's time to head on up the trail again.

"Some game that turned out to be," says Evan.

"Right, some game," I mumble.

For a while, I watch the line ahead of me. As usual, the gaps are widening. Twice I have to stop the troop to let us catch up.

Sometime after the second stop, I've fairly well sorted out

what happened in the match game. There was no reserve. When the kids downstream in the balanced model got behind, they had no extra capacity to make up for the loss. And as the negative deviations accumulated, they got deeper and deeper in the hole.

Then a long–lost memory from way back in some math class in school comes to mind. It has to do with something called covariance, the impact of one variable upon the others in the same group. A mathematical principle says that in a linear dependency of two or more variables, the fluctuations of the variables down the line will fluctuate around the maximum deviation established by any preceding variables. That explains what happened in the balanced model.

Fine, but what do I do about it?

On the trail, when I see how far behind we are, I can tell everyone to hurry up. Or I can tell Ron to slow down or stop. And we close ranks. Inside a plant, when the departments get behind and work-in-process inventory starts building up, people are shifted around, they're put on overtime, managers start to crack the whip, product moves out the door, and inventories slowly go down again. Yeah, that's it: we run to catch up. (We always run, never stop; the other option, having some workers idle, is taboo.) So why can't we catch up at my plant? It feels like we're always running. We're running so hard we're out of breath.

I look up the trail. Not only are the gaps still occurring but they're expanding faster than ever! Then I notice something weird. Nobody in the column is stuck on the heels of anybody else. Except me. I'm now stuck behind Herbie.

My guess is that Herbie, unless he's trying very hard, as he was before lunch, is the slowest one in the troop. I mean, he seems like a good kid and everything. He's clearly very conscientious—but he's slower than all the others. (Somebody's got to be, right?) So when Herbie is walking at what I'll loosely call his "optimal" pace—a pace that's comfortable for him—he's going to be moving slower than anybody who happens to be behind him. Like me.

At the moment, Herbie isn't limiting the progress of anyone

except me. In fact, all the boys have arranged themselves (deliberately or accidentally, I'm not sure which) in an order that allows every one of them to walk without restriction. As I look up the line, I can't see anybody who is being held back by anybody else. The order in which they've put themselves has placed the fastest kid at the front of the line, and the slowest kid at the back of the line. In effect, each of them, like Herbie, has found an optimal pace for himself. If this were my plant, it would be as if there were a never-ending supply of work—no idle time.

But look at what's happening: the length of the line is spreading farther and faster than ever before. The gaps between the boys are widening. The closer to the front of the line, the wider the gaps become and the faster they expand.

You can look at it this way, too: Herbie is advancing at his own speed, which happens to be slower than my potential speed. But because of dependency, my maximum speed is the rate at which Herbie is walking. My rate is throughput. Herbie's rate governs mine. So Herbie really is determining the maximum throughput.

My head feels as though it's going to take off.

Because, see, it really doesn't matter how fast any one of us can go, or does go. Somebody up there, whoever is leading right now, is walking faster than average, say, three miles per hour. So what! Is his speed helping the troop as a whole to move faster, to gain more throughput? No way. Each of the other boys down the line is walking a little bit faster than the kid directly behind him. Are any of them helping to move the troop faster? Absolutely not. Herbie is walking at his own slower speed. He is the one who is governing throughput for the troop as a whole.

In fact whoever is moving the slowest in the troop is the one who will govern throughput. And that person may not always be Herbie. Before lunch, Herbie was walking faster. It really wasn't obvious who was the slowest in the troop. So the role of Herbie—the greatest limit on throughput—was actually floating through the troop; it depended upon who was moving the slowest at a particular time. But overall, Herbie has the least capacity for walking. His rate ultimately determines the troop's rate.

We pass a trail marker. This is the mid-point of the hike. Five mile to go.

I check my watch. It's 2:30 p.m. We left at 8:30 a.m. So subtracting the hour we took for lunch, that means we've covered five miles . . . in five hours?

The demand was for us to cover ten miles in five hours, and we've only done half of that. Inventory is racing out of sight. The carrying costs on that inventory would be rising. We'd be ruining the company.

But there really isn't much I can do about Herbie. Maybe I could put him someplace else in the line, but he's not going to move any faster. So it wouldn't make any difference.

Or would it?

"HEY!" I yell forward. "TELL THE KID AT THE FRONT TO STOP WHERE HE IS!"

The boys relay the call up to the front of the column.

"EVERYBODY STAY IN LINE UNTIL WE CATCH UP!" I yell. "DON'T LOSE YOUR PLACE IN THE LINE!"

Fifteen minutes later, the troop is standing in condensed line. I find that Andy is the one who usurped the role of leader. I remind them all to stay in exactly the same place they had when we were walking.

"Okay," I say. "Everybody join hands."

They all look at each other.

Then I take Herbie by the hand and, as if I'm dragging a chain, I go up the trail, snaking past the entire line. Hand in hand, the rest of the troop follows. I pass Andy and keep walking. And when I'm twice the distance of the line-up, I stop. What I've done is turn the entire troop around so that the boys have exactly the opposite order they had before.

"Now listen up!" I say. "This is the order you're going to stay in until we reach where we're going. Understood? Nobody passes anybody. Everybody just tries to keep up with the person in front of him. Herbie will lead."

So we start off again. And it works. Everybody stays together behind Herbie. I've gone to the back of the line so I can keep tabs, and I keep waiting for the gaps to appear, but they don't. In the middle of the line I see someone pause to adjust his pack straps. But as soon as he starts again, we all walk just a little faster and we're caught up. Nobody's out of breath. What a difference!

"Mr. Rogo, can't we put somebody faster up front?" asks a kid ahead of me.

"Listen, if you guys want to go faster, then you have to figure out a way to let Herbie go faster," I tell them.

Then one of the kids in the rear says, "Hey, Herbie, what have you got in your pack?"

Herbie stops and turns around. I tell him to come to the back of the line and take off his pack. As he does, I take the pack from him—and nearly drop it.

"Herbie, this thing weighs a ton."

I open it up and reach in. Out comes a six-pack of soda. Next are some cans of spaghetti. Then come a box of candy bars, a jar of pickles, and two cans of tuna fish. Beneath a rain coat and rubber boots and a bag of tent stakes, I pull out a large iron skillet. And off to the side is an army-surplus collapsible steel shovel.

"Okay, let's divide this stuff up," I say. "Herbie, look, you've done a great job of lugging this stuff so far. But we have to make you able to move faster," I say. "If we take some of the load off you, you'll be able to do a better job at the front of the line."

Andy takes the iron skillet, and a few of the others pick up a couple of the items I've pulled out of the pack. I take most of it and put it into my own pack, because I'm the biggest. Herbie goes back to the head of the line.

Again we start walking. But this time, Herbie can really move. Relieved of most of the weight in his pack, it's as if he's walking on air. We're flying now, doing twice the speed as a troop that we did before. And we still stay together. Inventory is down. Throughput is up.

The time is now five o'clock and we have arrived. This means that after relieving Herbie of his pack, we covered about four miles in two hours. Herbie was the key to controlling the entire troop.

For more information on Eli Goldratt and his current projects visit www.eligoldratt.com

For information on other TOC books please visit our web site: www.northriverpress.com

For more information on the Theory of Constraints visit: www.goldratt.com

THE ASSOCIATED PRESS

STYLEBOOK AND LIBEL MANUAL

Fully Revised and Updated

Including Guidelines on
 Photo Captions
 Filing the Wire
 Proofreaders' Marks
 Copyright

Norm Goldstein, Editor

Addison-Wesley Publishing Company

Reading, Massachusetts   Menlo Park, California   New York
Don Mills, Ontario   Wokingham, England   Amsterdam   Bonn
Sydney   Singapore   Tokyo   Madrid   San Juan
Paris   Seoul   Milan   Mexico City   Taipei

Many of the designations used by manufacturers and sellers to distinguish their products are claimed as trademarks. Where known, those designations appear in this book with initial capital letters (i.e., Clorox).

Library of Congress Cataloging-in-Publication Data

The Associated Press stylebook and libel manual / editor, Norm Goldstein — Fully revised and updated.

      p. cm.
   ISBN 0-201-62704-3 (pbk.)
    1. Journalism—Style manuals.   2. Libel and slander—United States. I. Goldstein, Norm. II. Associated Press.
   PN4783.A83   1994
   808′.06607—dc20

Cover design by Hannus Design Associates

Set in 10-point Century Schoolbook

3 4 5 6 7 8 9 -CRS-97969594
Third printing, October 1994

This Addison-Wesley book is published by arrangement with The Associated Press
50 Rockefeller Plaza
New York, NY 10020

All inquiries about style guidelines should be addressed to the AP.

Addison-Wesley books are available at special discounts for bulk purchases by schools, corporations, and other organizations. For more information, please contact:
   The Corporate, Government, and Special Sales Department
   Addison-Wesley Publishing Company
   Reading, MA 01867
   1-800-238-9682